WOMEN'S WILD OATS

ESSAYS ON THE RE-FIXING OF MORAL STANDARDS

C. GASQUOINE HARTLEY

1st WORLD
LIBRARY
Literary Society

Women's Wild Oats

C. Gasquoine Hartley

© 1st World Library, 2007
PO Box 2211
Fairfield, IA 52556
www.1stworldlibrary.com
First Edition

LCCN: 2007923757

Softcover ISBN: 978-1-4218-4240-0
Hardcover ISBN: 978-1-4218-4142-7
eBook ISBN: 978-1-4218-4338-4

Purchase *"Women's Wild Oats"*
as a traditional bound book at:
www.1stWorldLibrary.com/purchase.asp?ISBN=978-1-4218-4240-0

1st World Library is a literary, educational organization
dedicated to:

- Creating a free internet library of downloadable ebooks

- Hosting writing competitions and offering book publishing
  scholarships.

Interested in more 1st World Library books? contact:
literacy@1stworldlibrary.com
Check us out at: www.1stworldlibrary.com

1st World Library Literary Society

Giving Back to the World

"If you want to work on the core problem, it's early school literacy."

- James Barksdale, former CEO of Netscape

"No skill is more crucial to the future of a child, or to a democratic and prosperous society, than literacy."

- Los Angeles Times

"Literacy... means far more than learning how to read and write... The aim is to transmit... knowledge and promote social participation."

- UNESCO

"Literacy is not a luxury, it is a right and a responsibility. If our world is to meet the challenges of the twenty-first century we must harness the energy and creativity of all our citizens."

- President Bill Clinton

"Parents should be encouraged to read to their children, and teachers should be equipped with all available techniques for teaching literacy, so the varying needs and capacities of individual kids can be taken into account."

- Hugh Mackay

To MY HUSBAND AND MY SON

CONTENTS

INTRODUCTORY

WOMAN'S CARNIVAL

"To the hungry soul every bitter thing is sweet."

—Prov. xxvii. 7.

The sudden collapse of the war left us in a daze. After the years of inhuman strain it was hard to ease off tension to the almost forgotten conditions of peace. I recall that ever to be remembered day, November 11th, 1918—Victory Day. In the early hours before noon I was in London, and my young son was with me. Everywhere was an atmosphere of anxiety, an unusual stillness. Men in little groups of two and three stood here and there, soldiers in larger numbers loitered or walked slowly along the pavements; girls and women waited at the doors of business houses and shops, where inside nobody seemed attending to the few customers. Everyone was waiting; there was an expectancy so great and so stirring that ordinary life had stopped. The last hour seemed endless in its slow passing. I do not remember ever to have experienced the same anxious tension, which was felt so strongly by us all that, in a way I cannot explain, we seemed to gain liberation from ourselves, and, losing individuality, were brought to share a universal impulse. The colossal importance of that hour made itself felt.

Then at last the peace guns sounded. We knew the armistice had been signed: Germany had accepted the terms offered by the Allies. The fear of utter misery was lifted: the war was over. The streets filled as if by magic, sellers of newspapers appeared, nobody knew from where, and were besieged. As the news spread, a delirium of enthusiasm caught the people. There never was such a day, and there never can be such a day again. From noon onwards in ever increasing numbers the streets were thronged with people. Strangers who had never set eyes on one another before rejoiced together as sisters and brothers. Heedless of rain, and mud, and slush, Londoners turned the city into a carnival of joy. Then as the hours advanced the fun grew wilder. People linked hands and danced, and—maddest of all—indulged in wild "ring of roses" around lamp-posts and in the centers of the great thoroughfares. From the Strand and into the West End and beyond was one packed concourse of people, a never-ending stream spread from pavement to pavement across the way, in processions, in pairs, in groups, in taxi-cabs, on the top of taxi-cabs, in and on and all over motor-omnibuses, hanging to the backs of cabs, on great munition lorries—everywhere clustering and hanging like swarming flies. There were soldiers, crowds of Dominion boys, young officers and privates, old men and young men from civil life, and thousands upon thousands of women and girls of every age and representative of every class.

It was the women that I noticed most: they were wilder than the men, making more noise, cheering, shouting and singing themselves hoarse, dancing and romping themselves tired. Quite undisguisedly the soldiers were led by them. It was Woman's Carnival as well as Victory Night.

It is very hard to find words to speak of what I felt. The

C. Gasquoine Hartley

universal gladness was intoxicating, and yet, none the less, as I watched and noted, the scene was a spectacle that for me at least, was shot strangely with apprehension, almost with pain, certainly with anger and regrets, with aspects unaccountably sad. I witnessed many incidents I am tempted to record, but events passed so quickly, and I do not wish to generalize rashly. One thing I noticed was the great number of women and girl smokers. The woman without a cigarette was almost the exception. There was no attempt at concealment. But what impressed me was the way of holding and smoking the cigarette with an awkwardness that proclaimed the novice. Quite plainly the majority of these girls were smoking not at all because they desired to smoke, but for a lark. A little thing, you will say, very harmless, and possibly you are right, and yet it is the straw which reveals the direction of the wind.

In all the riotous merriment there seemed to lurk the urgency of unsatisfied wants. These instabilities and shadows did not darken the whole prospect, it may be that they intensified the pageant; London was, indeed, very wonderful that evening. Yet all the foolish and ugly incidents, petty and grave alike, of which I could not fail to be aware, came to me with an effort of challenge as something not to be ignored, but steadily to be inquired into, as an imperative call for effort and courage, a spur once again to take up my pen and write to warn women.

My thoughts turned back over the last long four-and-a-half years—years of struggle, of violent disorders, anxiety and pain. That time was finished. Thanks to our dead! Honor to our great dead! The spectacle before me became wider and richer and deeper, more charged with hope and promise....

Bang! Laughter and harsh screaming as a rocket shot up starring the dark evening heavens with its clustering balls of colors. In many parts of the city, long obscured, lamps were lighted; row upon row of little electric globes of white and red and blue appeared, and the unaccustomed blaze infected the revelers. It gave a fresh impetus to shouting; it was like removing the curtain from some great, long-darkened mirror. The fun grew boisterous. At this corner there were cheers for the Prime Minister, at the next for Foch and Haig, and Beatty and the Grand Fleet, and for France and America. Numbers did not know what exactly they cheered; it did not matter, it gave an excuse for noise. Much noise was needed to keep up the revel and convince everyone that everybody was happy.

Unceasingly the violent merry-making went on. Hoot! and an immense motor-wagon, crowded with singing girls, blowing hooters, wildly waving flags, and followed by a trail of taxi-cabs like a gigantic wobbling tail, each one laden with ten, twenty, and even more soldiers, charged down a side street and urged its right of way brutally through the crowd.

It seemed to me that the whole spirit and quality of the reveling was summarized. A rabble of distractions sought to sway me hither and thither. Now, I watched a company of girls dancing with young officers to the accompaniment of a barrel organ, then a group singing, and another group playing some round game that I did not know; now it was some Tommies surrounded by a group of screaming girls. In one group a woman was carrying a baby, and a tiny child dragged at the hand of another girl, crying drearily, and no one noticed. Boys were kicking about boardings that had been torn from the statues in Trafalgar Square. The noise became more and more deafening.

Did anyone realize at all the colossal importance of that day? This hour of supreme thanksgiving, the most glorious of all days in the history of the world, was passing in a delirium of

C. Gasquoine Hartley

waste. For there was no joy, only a great pretense and noise.

In this medley the sense of the present tended to disappear. Victory Night, by some fantastic transformation, to me became terrible with menace. All the jostling, excited people, and especially the disheveled women and the crowds of rioting girls, appeared as tormented puppets, moving and capering, not at all from will and desire of their own, but agitated violently and incessantly by some hidden hand, forced into playing parts they did not want to play, saying words they had no wish to speak, cutting antics for which they had no aptitude or liking. Cruelties lurked everywhere, waiting in the confused mummery. Reality was being left and with it the practical grasp of those powerful simplicities that alone can guide life through confusion. I felt this with stinging certainty. Everyone seemed playing a part, goaded with the urgency of seeking an escape from themselves.

But must life always go on in the same way? Surely our great dead point us through all these pretenses into the future? Dead compelling hands, insisting with irritable gestures that this failure of life should cease, and cease forever.

A thousand serried problems seemed to be pressing on me at once. My young son was angry at my sadness, but it was the biting consciousness of his presence that ruled my mood. This world was *his* world; this England *his* England; this London was *his* London and that of all children. It was for them that the failure mattered. So I thought, tormented, tortured with pain and impatience.

Leaving the Strand, we turned down one of the narrow streets near to the Savoy Hotel, I forget which one it was, and walked to the Embankment. We came out not far from Charing Cross Bridge and looked down over the long sweep of the water. The evening sky was a dull gray, almost black, but the rain had ceased to fall, and just then above us there was a break as if the absent moon was working to cut the clouds adrift. A kind of luminous darkness closed around us. It was beautiful. The massed buildings rose a blurred outline between the river and the sky like great beasts crouching and ready to spring, while through the steel-black circlings of the bridge row after row of lights sparkled and glowed, and blurs of color, amber to warm orange, splashed upon the river. On the other side, behind us, the big hotels all were lighted, and the unaccustomed illumination appeared to give too full a flood of light to be quite real. Ever and anon rockets shot up into the gray and fell in burning rain, and every color was reflected in diminishing shades, above in that one luminous patch of sky, and below in the pallid, rippled water. Yes, the scene was beautiful, perfect as a dream-city one could desire; all the elements "composed" in the painter's sense, and in arrogance of soul I felt that the beautiful effect had been arranged for me: that it was like a faultless piece of scene-painting, only there is no artist who could paint it.

I watched in silence as my son talked at my side. Here there was almost no noise; reports of motors and the harsh clang of shouting echoed, but in the distance. After the crowds we had left, the wide roadway appeared deserted, and the quiet made it easy for me to urge myself past my despair. One moment at least I had in which I was conscious again of a spirit and quality in life; the immense forces working on while the city rioted its victory. But it all goes so slowly— not fast enough!

The night became darker, the gray rift in the clouds narrowed and closed, a few great drops of rain fell heavily. Around us the air blew chill, the trees, whose points stood out jet black among the sweeping line of the still shrouded Embankment lamps, murmured with innumerable angry voices as the wind

C. Gasquoine Hartley

cut through them, the bitter wind that rises before rain. My mood shivered under the loneliness that marks the end of all perfect things.

Afterwards we walked up Villiers Street to the Strand Station, and witnessed a little longer the riot of pretended joy. Now, the fun had grown more boisterous, or so it appeared to me in contrast with the quiet we had left. A seething mass—women and girls and soldiers linked arms in arms charged down the street, blocking the station entrances, shouting, beating rattles and tins for drums, making the most deafening noise. Must we go on past or through them all? Yes, and it was for me a necessary lesson, perhaps, for trying to snatch too much for myself by getting away—and forgetting. I had wanted to shirk, now I was forced back to attention.

How clearly I recall that crowd! It took much time to get our train, and, as we waited, almost unconsciously I began to take mental notes of what I saw. Soon my interest was fastened. I observed individuals with quickened attention from the very sharpness of my disillusionment. Incidents burnt themselves into my memory, not in themselves of great importance, but surely significant. I was being dragged back face to face with many questions difficult to solve. What impressed me sharply was the unhappy faces of almost all those wildly excited girls. To my fancy each one was hiding from herself, and hiding also from everyone else. One girl, in particular, I remember, a lank figure, brightly dressed and her head adorned by a wreathed Union Jack, whirling lean arms in an ecstasy of irritability, her shrill voice mounting from scream note to scream note. A sickness of soul cried from her restless over-taxed body. She was but one unit of a whole rowdy company. Even this night was used by them to grab at something to fool men—to smother God in their hearts. Just a play, a pretense, yes, a pretense of power, especially that; they had no thought beyond excitement, and that to me seemed only the first step. I could not believe that the new freedom, the new England would be made by such women. Their make-believe merriment, all this riotous celebrating of the world's stupendous Victory—what, after all, was it? And for me the desolate answer "Waste!" rang out from the unceasing noise.

"Surely this squandering of Woman's gift, this failure of herself must cease now that peace has come!" The cry broke wordless from me. I understood the reality of my fear. I knew the peril to the future. It is the problem of unstable woman, clamorous and devouring, that cries aloud for solution.

C. Gasquoine Hartley

FIRST ESSAY

THE PROSPERITY OF FOOLS

WHICH TREATS OF WAR WORKERS, AND THE CHANGES THAT HAVE COME IN WOMEN'S IDEALS

"The turning away of the simple shall slay them, and the prosperity of fools shall destroy them."—Prov. i. 32.

I

I have lying upon my study table, on the chairs and even spreading over upon the floor, a heaped-up litter of documents. Board of Trade inquiries, Government reports, newspaper cuttings, recent books, articles from the reviews and popular magazines—all dealing, in one manner or another, with women's labor and their position as workers in the immediate past and in the future. Woman, eternally surprising, has established her power in new fields.

During the five war years a revolution has taken place in the industrial position of women. But the war was not the cause of the revolution. It only afforded an opportunity for forces to display themselves which already were in action. It hurried women forward, running at top speed, along paths where before their feet had slowly walked. War hastened the action of forces existing already. The wage-earning woman came in with the forties with the factory system, and every year she has increased in numbers, but during the five years of war her ranks have gained an enormous influx; moreover, a different class of girls and women have come to seek different kinds of work. And what marks the permanent importance of this is that a change of occupations has brought with it a startling change of behavior and outlook.

Just as the militarist has regarded war, not as a means of preventing the enslavement of peoples and their subjection to foreign rule, but rather as in itself a source of virtue and blessing, of progress and civilization; so too the feminist teachers have told us, not that the entrance of women into munition works was necessary to enable our country to arm for its terrible war, but have hailed the successive appearances of women in factories, foundries, and railway-stations as in itself a great step forward; as a goal long strived for that has been gained. What has been going on is a continuance of the process by which women are led more and more to escape from any specialization of function and are brought into competition with men in every kind of occupation. Now, let us be clear about it: this is a process which makes the excitement and experience and possible good of the individual woman outweigh in importance the safeguarding of the perpetual stream of man. A confusion of values has led women astray. Being a woman _is_ a handicap. For the true carrying out of the duties of the wife and mother physical and mental quiet and sound nerves are needed. The industrial field has become the ideal place of action for the feminists, who persistently romanticize the independent commercial or industrial career, trampling heedlessly on the wisdom of the past, bent on living their own little lives and all that kind of egoistic futility; holding up as admirable cheap achievements in the hell of modern

C. Gasquoine Hartley

competitive, beggar-your-fellow-worker, sell-at-a-profit industrialism; blackening as sacrifice, as a limiting of character,
woman's service to her husband and her children, her work in
the home and in the nursery.

I tell you women everywhere among us are being starved of
sacrifice and service. Sacrifice lives in the soul of a woman,
and not alone in the separate spirit of the individual woman
to whom it is communicated only through a losing of herself,
which marks her union with the greatest powers of life. It is,
I think, one of the most destroying tragedies of our industrial
society that women are denied this sustenance in a fixed and
regulated unison of sacrifice, are forced away from service to
life, excited to do violence to their deepest instinct, by
engaging in the deadly and futile rivalry, where the greatest
successfulness must bring to them the greatest destruction.

There has been much happening to bring fear. Something has
gone wrong with the women of this land. In saying this, I am
not forgetting the splendidness of their work; what I
complain of is that their womanly vision has failed. In
France, as is evident to all, the attitude of women has been
very different. The French women also worked hard during
the war to save their country, but they did not as our women
have done, *like war-work for its own sake.* They never
transferred their affections from their homes to the factories
of war, they were too certain of themselves, too content with
their power as women to do anything so foolish. What is the
explanation of this profound difference in attitude? Why has
the vision of English women failed? That is the question to
which we have to try to find an answer.

The great part played by women coming forward during the war to take the place of men called to the army is disclosed in a White Paper recently issued by the Board of Trade. Over a million and a half women offered their services, in addition to those already employed.[23:1] The increase has been the highest in the occupations in which comparatively few women were engaged before the war. In April, 1918, 701,000 women were working on munitions and 774,000 in other industrial government employment. A disturbing fact revealed (called, I note, in the Report an *interesting point!*) is the number of women who have been engaged in hard, laboring work. Before the war when the public discovered women doing very hard work, it excited indignation and pity. The women chain-makers of Craddock Heath, to cite one example, were accorded general commiseration. But during the war our feelings on the question would seem to have undergone a somewhat sudden transformation; a complete turn-round has taken place in our attitude. Heavy work done by women—foundry work, for instance, *demanding great expenditure of physical strength*[24:1] has excited admiration and *become an important factor of the industrial situation.* A glamour of patriotic war service, added to the lure of high wages, has been thrown like a cloak of romance over such exhibitions of female power. They became victories of female will over female weakness.

Certainly in many cases the work done was quite unsuitable for women. The employment of married women during long days of tiring work had inevitable results. Babies were neglected or births were deliberately prevented. This spendthrift folly will have to be paid for in the future.

Not that I believe that all apparently hard work to be on an equality of unfitness for women. Country work is generally healthful; though hard work it is restful to the nerves. Every kind of nerve-racking work as in factories, heavy weight-lifting, long standing, and the tending of machinery without any kind of human interest, must be detrimental to women. Certain employments, consecrated by custom as comparatively womanly, yet, in their nerve-exhausting details mean ill-health. Take, for an instance, the average shop-girl, or machine worker, with her whitened face, dragging steps and flattened figure: does she not show plainly that she is anaemic and wanting in vitality? On the other hand, to my eye the lift attendants on the tubes, the charming conductresses of the 'buses seem healthy, though their work has been done only recently by women. I would make the influence of an occupation on woman's health—considering first and as most important her primary biological function as a potential mother—the test of its womanliness. But the health of women will never be protected while we are content to accept the valuations and suffer the defilements of this commercial age.

III

Only this morning I have been reading the newly issued *Report of the War Cabinet Committee on Women in Industry*, a large book of 340 pages, packed with information, in particular as to "the increased employment of women owing to the development of automatic machinery." What I read fills me with dismay and indignation. I was not prepared—and I thought I was prepared for anything—for such blindness of outlook.

To prove this, let me quote directly from the Report. The Committee urges rightly the importance to the health of the workers of good food, clothing and domestic comfort, and the necessity of good wages to maintain this standard. But *why are these improved conditions recommended*? Listen to what is said:

> *Properly nourished women have a much greater reserve of energy than they have usually been credited with, and under suitable conditions they can properly and advantageously be employed upon more arduous occupation than has been considered desirable in the past, even when these involve considerable activity and physical strain....*

And a little further:

> *It is desirable that women's wide employment should be made permanent.*

In another passage the Committee report *that on piece work a woman will always beat a man.* And again further on: *On mass production she will come first every time.... Men will never stand the monotony of a fast repetition job like women;*

C. Gasquoine Hartley

they will not stand by a machine pressing all their lives, but a woman will.[27:1]

Nothing that I can say, or any writer could say, could be more vividly condemning than are these passages. They have filled me with so deep a protest that really I can hardly trust myself to write any comment. This is the ideal now set before us for the industrial woman "to stand by a machine pressing all her life." I ask, Is it for this that the sons of these women have died? Marriage is spoken of as "one of women's industrial drawbacks," "it makes her less ambitious and enterprising."

Now, I do not wish to be unfair. The questions involved are, I know, immense and many-sided. There can be no easy dismissal of this valuable Report in condemnation. Mrs. Sidney Webb's minority Report[28:1] in particular is valuable; and in many ways the findings of the Committee are excellent. Everyone must agree with the wise recommendations as to the reduction of the hours of work and better conditions of labor. They are in advance of anything hitherto proposed. The popular formula of "equal pay for equal work" or more correctly "equal value," is accepted. If women are to do men's work, obviously they ought to be paid men's wages. Other very commendable recommendations concern pensions for widowed, deserted or necessitous mothers (I should add unmarried mothers). State payment is advised for the entire cost of the lying-in-period as the only way to ensure births under satisfactory conditions to the child and the mother. All this is just and good. If the state desires women to remain in industrial occupations, it is some gain that help should be given them, when for a few weeks they go from the factory to do their own work and bear children. Yet, after all, is there not something ridiculous, yes, and also disgraceful, in such a compromise. We leave a woman "to stand by a machine pressing all her life" (a work of monotony, so nerve-exhausting and soul-deadening that no man will do it), and then we pay her a small sum to enable her to bear an enfeebled child. Afterwards we send her back to the factory and open State creches and nursery-schools to rid her of the responsibilities and joys of bringing up her child. Such miserable makeshifts for fitting motherhood could be acceptable only in an industrially ruled society, where the simple belief would seem to be that *a woman can do everything that men won't do—and their own work as well.*

C. Gasquoine Hartley

IV

Let us be honest. Do we care for the cherishing of children? Do we want to preserve the health and help mothers? Are we really concerned with the prevention of our high infantile death-rate, with all the futile suffering without any sense of purpose or compensation that it must entail to children and to mothers? Let us pray to care more passionately, to see a vision of motherhood such as will force us to act differently; a vision which, as when the mists clear away among the mountains, will show a wide world lit by the sun. It would not then be difficult for us to know what to do; we should decide unhesitatingly as to the mother in industry, that *she ought not to be there.*

V

Many facts combine in acclaiming our indifference; all of which show our distressing inability to take a wide view of social problems with our commercially blinded eyes. We look at everything, even the nation's children, through spectacles of gold. I cannot wonder at our endless sicknesses and crime.

A small paper-backed book is now lying upon my desk. It is an inquiry most carefully made by the Minister of Reconstruction into the conditions of juvenile employment during the war, and, to me at any rate, it is pitiless in its revelation of our failure in this period of stress in knowing how to live.

It would be difficult, indeed, to find a more complete condemnation of what we have been allowing to go on in our factories and workshops. The Report reveals an intolerable neglect, a reckless betrayal of young lives that not even the emergency of war can sanction.[31:1]

Mark what the report tells us:

> *Unless those most competent to judge are mistaken, in the generation which entered industry between 1914 and 1918 vitality has been lowered, morale undermined, and training neglected....*

> *For three years numbers of young persons have been exposed to almost every influence which could impair health, undermine character and unfit them, both in body and mind, for regular industry and intelligent citizenship.*

And this passage also:

C. Gasquoine Hartley

From the point of view of the community, the adolescent worker is a potential parent and a potential citizen ... there is no doubt whatever what course of action should be prescribed by consideration for the interests of the nation. It would be to subordinate the employment of young persons for their immediate utility to their preparation for more effective work as men and women.... The danger is not that there may, in the present, be too few adolescent laborers, but that there may be too many, and that as a result there may in the future be too few healthy and well trained adult workers and intelligent citizens.

The profit-seeking employer, the patriotic maker of munitions, considers output: he does not think of the girls' or the boys' future, of the adult employment for which they are being prepared, or not prepared, or if the occupation leads, as so often is the case, to a blank wall. No kind of concern is shown of the degree in which the occupation enlarges the interests of the growing minds, or fritters them away and leaves for a later use nothing but a dead machine, capable only of spasmodic excitement; does not think of the effect of long hours or of large wages and their consequent premature freedom from home restraints on character.

The last mentioned evil has been greatly accentuated by the absence of soldier fathers. The indictable offenses committed by the young have increased markedly during the war, and surely we are responsible for this lapse of children into crime.

We have permitted heavy and nerve-exhausting work to be done in just the years when the adolescent was making the always difficult passage of the boy to the man, of the girl to the woman. And for this reason their suppressed, not-understood, thwarted instincts have broken out in unpleasing and often dangerous ways. Is it any wonder if in such circumstances boys turn to petty robberies and other unsocial acts, while girls display some of the less estimable characteristics of the prostitute?

Our ideal is to ignore sex in industry; to deny the strong and necessary separations that nature's wisdom places as barriers between boy and girl, between man and woman. We make our sons and daughters compete in education and in industry. No doubt education and industry are ill-fitted for males, but at any rate they were intended for males. Intellectually inferior to the boy or the man, the girl or woman is not. She is exasperatingly observant, often understands character with unconsidered quickness, feels spontaneously; but it does not follow that there is any value for her in the collection of dead facts, stored by abstract-minded professors—all the futile things we call education, which show in every direction the most coarse lack of understanding of the needs of the child and of life. And the girl suffers more than the boy, for the girl-student does as she is told much more conscientiously than boys. Similarly in industry: tapping or pushing at a machine until she taps or pushes on in her dreams; all the more monotonous kinds of machine-tending will wear feminine nerves, naturally more irritable than those of men, more than the same work will wear the male nerves. Not that I believe in subordinating the worker of either sex to the machine. What I want to prevent is the same stupid sacrifice of girls and women in industry as has been permitted in the case of boys and men. There has been in our commercialized society no kind of effective tradition for the care and guidance of adolescent workers, and, there is no escaping from the condemning proofs of our neglect: there has been, and, indeed, is still going on, in many directions a vast range of betrayal and baseness in the way we have shirked our duties to the young. As the writer, from whose Report I have quoted, says, with a rather grim irony: "a strain has been put on the character of young persons which might have corrupted the integrity of a Washington and have undermined the energy of Samuel Smiles."

VI

The war is over, and with it the special and pressing need for women's and girls' work, but the consequences of the war period are far, indeed, from nearing their end. Following all the industrial confusion of the war, we are now facing the certainty of wide-spread unemployment among women and girls. We have condemned thousands of them to unemployment with the same thoughtlessness with which they were called into industry; and in the less skilled ranges of employment, the always existing competition between men and women and boys and girls is certain to be fiercely accentuated.

It is officially stated that the number of women and girls who took out-of-work donation policies during the period between the Armistice and February 14th was 633,318. Of these the large majority 630,874 were civilians, while 2444 belonged to the forces. Thousands of women and girls who during the war proved themselves most capable at engineering and wood-work are now ruled out of those occupations. There was a girl of twenty, for instance, at Loughborough who showed real genius at gauge-making, work that required accuracy to the ten thousandth part of an inch. Although she took to the work only during the war, she became so good that instead of being sent to a factory she was kept to instruct others. This is the type of girl who now has to seek other employment. There can be no question of the difficulties of the situation.

Many workers are holding out to get the same level of work and pay as they have left. Strongest of all is the aversion shown to domestic work: many girls who have been engaged on munitions during the war have thrown up their unemployment pay rather than again enter domestic service.

C. Gasquoine Hartley

Factory work has bitten into girl's lives; they do not want to do any other kind of work.

Visit one of the Women's Employment Exchanges, if you would wish to get to know these girls. The Exchange is usually a hall or large room where busy clerks are at work at long tables. At some Exchanges as many as 2000 to 2500 women and girls will be on the books. Once a week they receive their out-of-work pay; every alternate day they have to visit the Exchange to see what jobs are vacant. You may watch them pass in long queues from one table to another. A few of the women will probably carry babies, but the great majority will be young girls, showily dressed. You will hear the discordant murmur of their voices broken often by sharp giggles. The moving lines seem to go on and on unendingly. At one table the girls sign the register, at another they learn of vacancies. Some of the girls fail to go to the second table. An attendant, if you ask the cause, will tell you this is a frequent occurrence. The girls are punctilious in signing the register, which they must do to obtain the unemployment dole, but they are less particular about finding the work which will bring it to an end. At present they are content with the enjoyments of the streets and picture palaces. I have, on many different occasions, spoken to these workers: one case I may quote as typical of many. She was young, about twenty, I should think, and incredibly self-confident. Before the war she had been a tailor's needle hand earning 16s. a week; for the last two years she was inspecting fuses at a wage of 45s. a week. What was she now going to do? Neither she nor any of the other women to whom I have spoken seemed to have any clear realization of the fact that the change-over from war to peace industries by munition factories, with the return of many thousands of men, was bound to result in a serious excess supply of woman labor. I remember it was then, while I talked to this girl, that the first great suspicion stole into my heart. We have heard so much of the splendid conduct of the women and the wonderful way in which they have done the work of men, but the facts stand up stark. *Women have had a good time.* Now, they are going to struggle to keep it. These girls are vastly more rebellious than any women were five years ago.[38:1]

Look at the girl-workers you may see everywhere in such numbers to-day; they are of all ages and they belong to all classes of society. Watch them as they fight for an entrance into motor omnibuses and trams, as they crowd the station platforms. See them parading the streets in their unemployed hours; they are the companions of every soldier; they crowd the cinemas, music-halls, and theaters. Who has altered the fashions about every three months? and this has been going on in war time. Why, the munition workers and the forty-shilling-a-week girls. No longer was finery always bought out of men's earnings, but out of their own; put on to give some man a treat or to fire the envy of other girls. The factory girl has taken to silk stockings and fine lingerie and the lady to Balbriggan and calico.

The vast change that has come into the daily lives of women, possibly, in no direction is more startling than it has been in this matter of dress. Many shops which are near the factories where munition girls have been employed have organized war-clubs, in which, on payment of a small weekly sum, the girls could buy articles of attire far in advance even of their high wages. Shops festooned with furs of every description, where coats costing ten, twenty, and even thirty and more guineas, were frequently bought; shops whose windows were a clutter of tissue-like crepe-de-chine underclothes and blouses; boot-clubs and jewelry-clubs, these last, garish establishments, secure in the glamour of irresistible imitations—all have urged to extravagance and a madness for ornament.

C. Gasquoine Hartley

The West-end tradesmen and the shareholders of the big drapery shops have been chuckling and rubbing their hands. Dividends have sprung up to a figure they have never before reached. Never before has so much money been wasted on adornment.

Our young women have little thought beyond the present use of what they buy. But I believe that much of this extravagance—the delight in self-gratification which finds other expression in jazzing, in sweet-eating, in card playing, smoking and similar pleasures—is not so much the outcome of the thoughtlessness of youth as a way of escape from Self, a misdirected effort toward safety, unconscious no doubt, but terribly real.

Notice these girls. You will see them best in a walk down Oxford street or in Leicester Square, where, snared by each displayed window, they hover and cluster like wasps drawn to a trap of sweet food. All the biggest shops in London are devoted to women's clothes. Do you realize that? And it is not only that they are the biggest, but there are more of them than any other half a dozen trades put together—the only exception being the drink trade. During the war their number has multiplied, indeed in some districts shops have sprung up like mushrooms in the night.

There is a much deeper importance in this question of dress than usually is allowed. Irresponsible spending does encourage irresponsible living.

Almost everyone has at one time or another thought of some reform they would wish to be made in the society in which they live. Now, if I could have my choice as to any one reform I would choose to be done, it would be to make it illegal for a tradesman to display for sale any kind of wearing apparel, dress goods or articles connected with a woman's toilet, either in shop windows or inside the shops. Nothing must be shown to any customer until it is asked for. I do really believe this simple reform would do more to emancipate women, and, through their emancipation, to liberate men, than any other reform. We pray in our churches "lead us not into temptation," and everywhere we permit in our shops the display of goods to tempt the young and the foolish.

An orgy of adornment has been claiming a veritable sacrifice of comfort and health, possibly even of life. All-night vigils in search of bargains are frequent at the bi-annual sale-festivals. Policemen have to restrain the ardent votaries, as they press forward and struggle and fight to obtain entrance to certain shops, like caged animals fighting for food. Fashions are followed passionately and with little variety. Dark heads and golden heads have the hair bobbed or dressed in the same way, with the same plastered side-curls, and adorned with hats alarmingly alike, weighted with queer and polychrome ornaments of beads, wool, tassels, and I know not what, while the face beneath shows one color of yellowish white, the result of the excessive and unskillful use of cheap powder. In the snow and slush of the spring, I have seen girls dressed in a way fit only for the hottest indoor room. The gauze silk-stockings offering no protection to the tortured feet even when the boots and shoes were made of more than paper stoutness; while the fashionable woolen wrap, even the fur collar or coat could not counterbalance the danger to health from blouses, low-necked and fashioned of stuff scarcely thicker than cobwebs. Here and there the many girls, beautiful in quiet uniforms, have served to throw into sharper contrast the absurdities of the dress of their sisters.

I ask myself how this taste for spending money on dress and ornament—a taste very little different from the instinct which causes savages to adorn their half-naked bodies with feathers, beads and shells—is to be satisfied when women's wages fall? There would seem to be nothing too useless or too expensive for girls to buy. Work has failed in teaching them the simple lesson that not only is it wrong to waste money, but it is wrong to waste labor for the gratification of whims. We are having the need for economy preached and shouted at us from every quarter. Surely it is right to think about this wild spending on adornment, and give at least a few glances to the future.

What is likely to happen now when the full years of war change to empty years of peace? No longer able to spend in the way to which their high wages have made them accustomed, girls will seek to get presents from men; they will want excitement and the dress and pleasures to satisfy that need, also to hold the envy of their friends. This must lead to prostitution. The weaker sort of girl will prefer to sell her body rather than go back to a humdrum life of drudgery in back-kitchens. It is well that we should remember that, if women are to suffer through men's passions, men will suffer no less from women's greed.

I desire to be quite fair. Almost all girls, I think, are better looking since 1914, more confident, more brightly attractive; sometimes they are deliriously gay, more often cheaply aggressive and noisy. Yet, at other times, they seem deadened and slow in response. None of them are shy. Their eyes say things that are hard to read; they exhibit no end of energy, but there is a curious kind of contradiction—a confusion and difficult defiance, with much nervous weakness. I can find no steadfast happiness.

I would ask my readers, as often I have asked myself, a question: Have these modern girls not lost much of the tender, waiting, indefiniteness of youth? I have seen so many among them who, to me at least, appear at odds with the world, and their passionate, unbalanced and over-excited natures. Their faces at sixteen, fifteen, and even at fourteen years, already are old, with hard confidence showing in the bold gaze, but no happiness. How many bear an expression of almost tired disappointment, a disappointment, not of the senses, but of the soul. And this expression is so common. To my eyes, girls far more and far oftener look alike now than formerly they did. So often they seem acting, struggling almost against something in themselves; something they don't understand that draws them into many bewildered actions. Can't you see, they are all so unconsciously dissatisfied, so unable to possess themselves in peace, that nothing they do matters? You will, I am sure, deny this statement. You will tell me again of the splendid work done by these girls and young women, you will speak of their recognition as citizens of the State, of how life has opened to them, and of the new liberty they have gained in so many directions. I do not mind. I care nothing for the liberty in outside things that leaves the soul in chains. I tell you they are dissatisfied because the soul of woman is crushed, unable to come up from its dark hiding, and breathe the sun and light to see that life is good. Why cannot the old faith come back? Why cannot it come back?

C. Gasquoine Hartley

VII

It is, of course, easy to write of these evils, the difficult thing is to find a remedy. Many attempts are being made; much discussion is taking place about the future position of women in industry; training is being given to adolescent girls; even schools for wives have been formed. The newly established Ministry of Health has wide schemes for maternity and child welfare. Never was so much expended to right things that are wrong. Yet, I cannot think the remedies offered are likely to be satisfactory.

Let me here pause for a moment to compare my view of the true remedy for the present unsatisfactoriness of women's lives, and the consequent wastage of baby lives, with those remedies now so commonly put forward by the reformers. I assert that women are trying in vain to transfer their affection from babies to machines, and to take care of their babies, if they have them, in the few hours left over after days seriously devoted to business. I will test the results in a way fairer to my opponents than to myself, comparing the effects of their method at its best with my system in circumstances little favorable to human life.

Bradford is a wealthy town: spending some L40,000 annually on the care of infants in a total population of 300,000. Its institutions and arrangements for this purpose are famous; its infant department, its graded municipal milk, its free-feeding for expectant mothers—all are as nearly perfect as is possible; and the men who have developed and direct its municipal system of protection for infants are well known for their ability and enthusiasm. The birth-rate is as low as Malthusians could desire. But all its care is but an attempt to lessen evils brought about by a wrong system; for the mothers of Bradford are not in their homes, but in woolen factories.

County Roscommon is a poor district in Ireland, with a primitive and superstitious population of agriculturists; the birth-rate is very high, and there is practically no public provision for the safeguarding of infant life. But its backward ignorant mothers tend and feed their babies after the manner of the earliest ages.

The infant death-rate is 135 in Bradford, and 35 in Roscommon.

You will see what I wish to make plain. Those whom I criticize are dealing with symptoms instead of working to remove the real cause of the disease. They work hard and achieve little. Of course their efforts are praiseworthy, and, under present conditions, frightfully necessary. But they are just about as lastingly useful as trying to mend a badly broken china cup at home with cheap cement. You know what happens: as soon as you succeed in getting two pieces to stick together another piece tumbles away, and, at last, if by excessive patience the work gets done and the cup is mended, the first shock of hot water makes all the pieces again fall apart. It is a solution that gives great opportunity of employment, one indeed that goes on forever; perhaps that is why it fascinates the child-like minds of the feminists. I want something very different.

I want a tradition of life to hand on to our daughters and to their daughters. We need a strongly deepened sense of womanly responsibility, wide-spread and universally accepted; an up-to-date sense, if you like that term. I have no fears of change. I would re-fix our moral standards more fearlessly than many who think me old-fashioned. But what I want to insist upon is this: *The standard of conduct must be fixed for women.* Our children want something settled, not everything left uncertain. Our morals (I do not mean our sexual morals only, but our whole ethical and social conduct) has become like a skein of wool that has been unraveled by a puppy. We want a firm broad way in which it is good and possible for all of us to walk without hurting one another, not the horrid scramble that to-day we accept as life.

The modern conception of personal rights is essentially individualistic, and has arisen only under industrial values of life; the result of its further application as a social criterion for women, must logically be exactly what it has been in the experience of the past century: a bitter and brutal struggle for self-aggrandizement, with the failures remorselessly crushed underfoot, and the very idea of a fixed common responsibility and common good for all forgotten or denied. My plea for women is, therefore, based not upon the notion of equal rights, but rather upon that of equal duties. Moral equality means equality in the will to serve—not self, but all. And the practical correlative of this conception must be a social organization which secures equalities of opportunity for service to women and men. The only rights I desire to claim for my sex are those necessary to the discharge of its own duties; the fulfillment of the instinctive maternal craving; the realization of the deepest impulses of a woman's nature.

The pitiless war of every individual against his, or her, fellow waged with gold or with steel, can never make life other than mean and empty. Women and men must learn again to regard themselves as part of a mightier whole, one of the human race, and, as we feel in moments of deeper insight, of the universe, which is a unity in spite of all the discords it contains.

It follows from this, that I am not greatly concerned with what any individual woman, or group of women, can do, or cannot do, should be encouraged to do, or be restrained from doing, in competition with men and with each other, but rather what is most right and worth while for all women, *as women*, to do. *I do not want freedom for each woman to do what she wants.*

You see, in my view of life, such freedom can lead only to a more degraded slavery. And because I am certain about this, I do not desire success for women in the blind struggle based on the doctrine (so fundamentally untrue in my opinion) of personal rights. A doctrine which results inevitably in separations, in hatreds, in disorders and struggling one with another. Unity of ideals and of conduct becomes impossible. The general life is driven about in this way or the other, directed by this purpose or by that, but always by individualistic principles, and not to serve the good of all, but by each person for his own, or her own, ends. How can order come out of such a way of life? Do you think you are going to improve things in the old selfish ways. I tell you the result can be nothing but a further failure of vision. The mountain heights become obscured by the mists going up from the damp valleys, and the soul loses its way.

FOOTNOTES:

[23:1] The statistics show the situation up to April, 1918.

[24:1] The words I have italicized are not mine, but are quoted from the Report.

[27:1] It is worth noting that, as far as I know, no word of protest has been made by women against these statements. The Report, since I wrote this chapter, has been widely commented on in the daily papers, in some of the weeklies, and in all the suffrage papers, but these passages have been passed over. Surely this is very significant.

[28:1] Since published by the Fabian Society as a small book.

[31:1] An excellent article on the Report, entitled "Demobilization of Juvenile Workers," by Miss L. B. Hutchins, appeared in the *Contemporary Review*, February, 1919.

[38:1] Since writing this, the Government, backed by the Labor Party, has passed its Pre-war Practices (Restoration) Bill, which will exclude women from many of the trades which they have entered during the war; trades in which they have done skilled work and received high wages. On August 15, The Sex Disqualification (Removal) Bill, after a promising early career, went by default.

SECOND ESSAY

THE COVENANT OF GOD

WAR MARRIAGES AND ROMANTIC LOVE, WHICH
CONTRASTS THE ENGLISH IDEAL OF PERSONAL
HAPPINESS IN MARRIAGE WITH THAT HELD BY
THE JEWS OF MARRIAGE AS A RACIAL DUTY.

"Which forsaketh the guide of her youth, and forgetteth
the   covenant of her God."—Prov. ii. 17.

I

A few weeks ago I read a book about a war-marriage,
entitled the "Wife of a Hero"; it was not a good novel, but
the situation it presented was of great interest. We witness
the manifold conflicts resulting from a marriage entered into
in haste and under superficial emotions, between a war-hero
and the more complicated type of modern woman—the
woman of brains and nerves, fastidious, intellectually
passionate and at the same time swayed by a sensuality,
which is neither acknowledged nor understood. Hence this
woman's marriage with a man, who, sufficiently a hero to die
magnificently (as a matter of truth he does not die and

C. Gasquoine Hartley

returns in the end to receive the Victoria Cross, but it was believed he was dead) was quite unfitted to live decently. You see, his ideals did not get any further than his vanity. In his view a woman—whether wife or mistress, it did not signify which she was—was only a chattel, an object to give enjoyment to him, in fact, a prostitute. He did not know he felt this, could not know it, in fact. It would have needed a revolution of his character to turn his vision to something other than himself. Neither did the wife realize her egoism, an egoism more agreeable certainly than was his, because on a less crude plane, but equally reprehensible, as spiritually barren and limited to Self as was that of the man.

Now, Miss Netta Syrett, the writer of the book, seems to be unaware of such a failure on the woman's part. All the blame is shoveled on to the hero, all the sympathy wrapped like a thick woolen cloud about the heroine. Miss Syrett is a great feminist. As we should expect, the marriage is broken in the Divorce Court. The returned and invalided hero, decorated with his Victoria Cross, seeks happiness with an earlier love, and a marriage is made of a frankly sensual character. Meanwhile the heroine finds a spiritual mate in the person of an old friend, and a second marriage is made. We are led to believe that all the wrong is set right. Now, I doubt this. I believe the cause which brought the first marriage to such painful disaster was not dependent only on the evident unsuitability of the partners to live with one another; the grossness of the man and the believed refinement of the woman need not necessarily have failed in finding happiness in union. No, the cause of failure was deeper, within themselves, dependent on the blind egoism of both the husband and the wife and their wrong understanding of the institution of marriage. I do not think that in either case the second marriages were likely to be much happier than the first marriage.

II

The love-story of to-day differs in one essential way from the love-story of yesterday. Yesterday's love story always ended with marriage bells; to-day's, which is a far harder love-story to write, begins with them. Earlier authors, in short, shirked the real problem of marriage, they ended where they should have begun. For the main difficulties do not lie in the period of falling in love, in the courtship or the honeymoon, but in the preservation of love after these passionate preliminaries are over.

Now, I would like to be able to say that the modern love-story affords a sure sign of a change that has taken place in our attitude towards marriage. I am not, however, at all certain. We talk a great deal, I fear, that is all. The innumerable tragedies of marriage among us to-day are witness to our failure; they have a far closer connection than often is recognized with the romantic and vulgar poverty of our point of view.

Our romances are slightly vulgar. Vulgarity is a sign of confusion and weakness of spirit. We still far too much associate romance with courtship and not with marriage; that is one reason English marriages so often are unhappy. "Thank God that our love-time is ended!" cried a north country bride on the day that marriage terminated her long engagement.

Now, I do not know whether this delightful story is true, but it does illustrate the attitude of many ordinary couples, whose love adventure ends at the very hour it should begin. Every true marriage ought to be a succession of courtships.

Love is not walking round a rose-garden in the sunshine; it's

C. Gasquoine Hartley

living together, growing together. And the honeymoon is as trifling as the *hors d'oeuvre* in comparison with wedded-love, and as unable to satisfy the deep needs of women and men. Falling in love, wooing, and honeymooning are a short and easy episode, but marriage is long and always difficult. And the finding and maintaining happiness is a definite achievement and not an accident, for *it is beyond accident*. It is the result of a steadfast ideal and a diligent cultivation.

III

Marriage has not escaped the general disturbances of the past five years. The causes are many and obvious. Man is generally guided, not directly by the automatic instincts, working through the lower nerve centers, but rather by ideas acting in the higher nerve centers of his brain. Instincts with him are not instinctive, but are checked and supervised by intelligence. Only when a great shock, a sudden fear or joy, occurs does the instinctive working replace the consciously planned action: the man or the woman find themselves speaking in an unaccustomed voice, saying what they did not know they would say; doing unaccustomed things, which they had never intended to do, sometimes they lose control of their body—they rage, their speech descends to inarticulate cries. Then the old system of instinctive response to the outer world, which generally is inactive and so imperceptibly becomes disused, becomes by the sudden generation of excessive emotion stocked with energy, so that it exceeds in power the energy of which the intelligence makes use. Impulses leap into being, and very often there is a sudden response to adventure and more primitive actions.

This is what the War did in many departments of life. Normal control, conventional standards, old careful habits of conduct, were broken through at a time of excessive emotionalism. The many hasty marriages were a sign of the nervous condition of the times. The customary criticisms of reason were not heard, or not until the emotional storm had subsided. This is, of course, a condition not infrequent in marriage; but now it was exaggerated; such marriages may not, unfortunately, bear the scrutiny of minds restored to sobriety.

We have called these war marriages real romances. But are

they? What does the husband know of the girl he has taken to be one with his own flesh? What does she know of him? Never have they had one real talk, never stood the test of a quarrel, never passed unexciting days with one another.

I want to labor that point. The most frequent causes of trouble in marriage are born of the daily fret of common living, of minor habits, of omissions and stupidities. Romantics may protest, but what most strains and tears our love are just trifles, so insignificant that rarely is their adverse action even noticed.

The safe and right consideration in any relationship that is to last into marriage is not only—are our persons agreeable to each other? But, can we live together and continue to love one another? It needs a lot of grit and a lot of duty to keep in love with daily life. But war turned men into heroes, while women thought the war was going to be so fine they could do anything to help; they wanted their share, each one to have a stake for herself, and the easiest way to gain this was the ownership of a soldier-lover. It prevented the feeling of "being left out." A new friendliness sprang up between the sexes. Advances were made, perfectly natural, but quite unusual; and the men in khaki and in blue found themselves diligently pursued, and it must be owned they liked it.

Thus many men have taken girls for wives who are everything they don't want their wives to be. There is no fitness of disposition and character, no unity of ideals, no passionate surrender of the Self in devotion, no fixed purpose of duty, no harmony in tastes or outlook. Such love must come to disaster; it is like a damp squib, it is never properly alight and fades out swiftly in noisy splutters. Then, when the first desire goes, no friend but an enemy is discovered.

A man falls in love very readily, and girls have used, quite unconsciously sometimes, very consciously in some cases, the man's undisciplined impulses for his own subjection. I need not recall incidents that all among us must have witnessed. I do not wish to pass any censure upon women. The sensualist within most of us is stronger than we women admit, and the primitive fact forces us to take risks, sending us headlong into a thousand dangers.

C. Gasquoine Hartley

IV

Can we ever find perfect love? Is it not like exercise of the body? You can develop it to a certain point, but not beyond without danger and very slowly with continued patient work. Do we not need exercise of the soul? I do not know. Often I feel I know nothing. To some men and women it is all simple enough, a woman is just a woman and a man is a man. The trouble begins when any woman becomes the one desired woman and any man the one desired man.

There is gain and development in this selective tendency of Love—and yet, if I am right, there is terrible danger lurking in the application of this egoistic spiritual view.

It is, little as we may believe it, this search for personal spiritual happiness that often so greatly endangers marriage. Searching always for this perfect mate, we must find a partner corresponding in every respect to our ideal. The man in Mr. Hardy's novel, "The Well Beloved," spent forty years in trying to do this, and his ultimate failure is typical of the experience of most of us. Fools and blind, we neither understand nor seek the cause of our failure. We are like little lost dogs searching for a master. We seek without ceasing some pilot passion to which we can surrender our heavy burden of freedom. The dry-rot destruction of this individualistic age has worm-eaten into marriage; we have sought to drown pain and the exhaustion of our souls, to fill emptiness with pleasure, to place the personal good in marriage above the racial duty, to forget responsibility, to arrogate for the unimportant Self, and, in so doing, inevitably we have turned away from essential things. Can't you see that we are so terribly tired of this search for something that we never find? Our adventures are the tricks of the child to cloud our eyes to our own emptiness and pain.

V

Marriage is not a religion to us: it is a sport.

I say this quite deliberately. I am sure we know better how to engage a servant, how to buy a house, how to set up in business—how, indeed, to do every unimportant thing in life better than we know how to choose a partner in marriage. We require a character with our cook or our butler, we engage an expert to test the drains of our house, we study and work, and pass examinations to prepare ourselves for business, but in marriage we take no such sensible precautions, we even pride ourselves that we do *not* take them.

We speak of *falling* in love and we *do fall*. There really is something ludicrous in our attitude. We English are everlasting children in an everlasting nursery; we so fiercely refuse seriousness towards the fundamental emotions. The conventions are sacred; nothing else matters. We stand for purity, which means with women ignorance, and with men silence and discretion.

Men and women of our earlier England were more natural. Our novelists then frankly said that every girl looked with special interest on a well-formed man. There was no conviction marking this as improper, "the baser side of love." We have grown more and more distorted and demagnetized from the natural needs of our nature. We try to cast discredit on our appetites and the body. We have lost the old firm tradition of marriage and its duties, and we have succeeded in putting nothing fixed in its place.

Now, I resent the romantic idea that marriage should be a hazardous mystery—at least to the woman. The more

C. Gasquoine Hartley

shrewdly girls can judge men and men can judge girls (not by mere talking and abstract discussion of sex problems, there has been too much of that kind of futility), but the more calmly the young lovers can find agreement with each other, the more simply they can accept the facts of marriage, the more chance there will be of permanency of affection.

The conventions of to-day are false, are bound up with concealments or with an equally untruthful openness. It does not, however, follow from this that mere destruction of the conventions will be enough; that everyone's unguided ignorance will lead to success and freedom. The *laissez faire* system is as false in the realm of marriage as it is in industry and economics. While equally false, as I have tried to show, is the too spiritual view of marriage that love can be found only in perfect harmony of character between the wife and the husband, and is independent of duty. It is true that love differs from lust in its deeper insight into the personality, deeper interest in the character, as opposed to the inexpressive smooth outline and "unbrained" physical beauty of the body. But character and intellect may be studied and loved as self-centeredly, as much with a view to the enjoyment of mental excitement, as the body itself. A wider distinction must be drawn before we can find guidance.

VI

Let us look now at a different, older and, as I think, much finer ideal of marriage, for by this means we may find out more clearly how very far we have wandered from happiness and freedom in marriage in our search for those very things.

It is the Jewish ideal of marriage that I wish to bring before you. And I would say first that the remarks I am offering are not gathered only from what I have read and been told by others. I have learnt them from my own experience, unconsciously and slowly, and even against my will. My marriage with a Jew has taught me the wide separation between the Jewish ideal of marriage and that which I had accepted: I cannot even try to say how much I have gained and learnt.

The English ideal of marriage is concerned with rights and the individual, the Jewish ideal is concerned with service and the race. Their theory of marriage is one of religious duty, and has much less to do with the accomplishments of passion; I think that is why Jewish marriages are so happy.

Modern writers on the Jewish point of view (such as Achad-ha-Am and Melamed) are agreed that the morality of the Jews is a collective rather than an individual morality, aiming at race preservation rather than individual development, practice rather than faith, the continuance and improvement of life rather than spiritual recompense. Consequently, wherever Jewish traditions retain their hold, the begetting and care of children must necessarily occupy the most important portion of life. Thus marriage is regarded as a duty to be undertaken by all, not as a pleasure to be indulged in or to be left dependent on the individual will. It is a sacred duty of parents to arrange a marriage for every child; marriage and the life of the home is still deeply

C. Gasquoine Hartley

religious; Jewish mothers do not go out to work in factories, they are more concerned with the service of the home than with anything outside of the home. They are very old-fashioned, and they are very happy: they consider barrenness the greatest possible misfortune.

Do you see the contrast I am trying to establish? The essence of the romantic ideal of marriage is at bottom an insupportable egoism—the seeking of happiness by the all too insistent Self—the forgetting of the ultimate values of life.

There are other modes of thought for Jewish women. The expression of her own individuality is not a matter to which she can attach supreme importance; rather is she unconsciously finding an escape from this burdening consciousness of individuality by ever seeking identification with her husband, with her children, with her home, with her own people and with God. She possesses the inestimable good of being bound by a great tradition. It is ever thus with those who are conscious of a sufficient inner life: the modern cry for individual freedom is but one result among many of the poverty of our lives.

The Westernized Jews, it is true, are more or less tainted with the errors of industrial communities. It is, of course, where the early marriages of the ghettoes prevail, where the married woman religiously covers her own hair with a wig immediately after marriage, where marriage, as I have said, is regarded as a duty, and love, therefore, is not considered to be of overwhelming importance, that the full difference between Jewish and Gentile traditions is seen.

This difference is partly due directly to religious influences. Christianity considers marriage as a concession to human wickedness and the continuance of the race a doubtful benefit. "A remedy for sin" as the English Prayer Book states with such delightful frankness. When I remember this Christian view of marriage, I am not surprised at the corruptions into which we have fallen; it is an atmosphere rich for the development of industrial values. The Jews have never fallen into this hateful denial of life. Judaism still considers it a command of God to increase and multiply: the unmarried life, not the married life, is regarded as sinful. The ascetic view of marriage, as well as the romantic view that love is everything, are both anti-Jewish.

The Jews, and, I think, even more strongly the women, can never be individualists. I must again emphasize this fact, for everything else depends upon it. Never can the Jewish wife and mother come to seek personal pleasure as the chief aim in marriage, or delight greatly in expressing her own individuality in spiritual union. She is not absorbed by her own joy or engrossed by her own sorrow. She is content to be married, and accepts any disadvantages that come from that state; she believes in her husband, in her children, and even if these fail her, she believes in her race, her religion, and the inheritance of her people: this gives her a center of gravity outside of herself. For thousands of years Jewish women have been taught the value of service; the dedication of the Self to an ideal. At the same time, they have been held firm to the realities of marriage by their worship. These two influences will, I believe, forever make it impossible for Jewish women in any numbers to accept the egoistic view of marriage and the duties of women that has been set up in England, as also in other European lands and in America, indeed wherever Self-assertion has been admitted as the ruling principle of life.

For these reasons the Jewess, with her special attitude toward marriage and to life, offers a picture of the deepest significance for the study of all industrial races. That is why I turn to her in the hope of making plain to us Western

C. Gasquoine Hartley

women our mistakes. She, in my opinion, can show us the path wherein alone in future we can find happiness.

The Jewish women have inherited the most perfect feminist ideal that as yet the world has known; an ideal of service within the home of which full life she is the high-priestess; an ideal turning to foolishness the false values of this industrial age. And this ideal of service, shared by all, gives to the most unlearned Jewish woman the priceless knowledge of an eternal truth: a truth that has to be learnt by each one among us before we can find happiness—that only by losing ourselves can we find the Self that is eternal. The Jewish woman learns this truth by living it.

The deep reasons of life lie beyond the realm of individual advantage. The Jewish spirit, pursuing its ends deliberately and wisely, demands of women and of men two different devotions. It asks of women devotion to men, to their children, to their homes; of men, devotion to ideals. Jewish women do not wait to ask if men are worthy, their thought is of service. They understand that in each devotion lies an equal glory, an equal joy, and an equal honor in the sight of God and of man.

There is so much more I would like to say. I would wish to show you something at least of the success with which religion among the Jews has been turned to domestic uses. No detail of the home life is left unhallowed. Even the poorest Jewish home is saved by its ceremonies from the degrading indifference to decency and tenderness, which is the terrible feature of the industrial homes of poverty. The sanctity of the home is an affectionate tradition linking the Jews through the ages with a golden chain. The purity of home life has fought and triumphed over all the unsanitary conditions of ghetto life.

I wish that the limits of my space allowed me to write in detail of these beautiful and happy services. The lighting of the Sabbath candles, the joyous festivals so attractive to our children, all are used to consecrate the daily life. The dietary laws may be said to be a religion of the kitchen. The description of the Virtuous Woman, from the book of Proverbs—the woman who "looks well to the ways of her household," whose clothing are "strength and majesty," who "laugheth at the time to come"—is appropriately read on Friday evenings by the master of the house to exalt the perpetual provident, charitable and joyous house-mistress. A true Jewish home must always be a beautiful place, because its duties are fixed by tradition and hallowed, by the symbols of God's dealing with His people in the past.

Abundant evidence is forthcoming of the honor that was always paid by the Jewish husband to his wife. His duties toward her are set forth in detail in the usual form of the *Ketubah*. In the body of that instrument he binds himself to work for her, and to honor her, to support and maintain her. The Talmudic sayings on this subject of the honor in which the wife is held and the husband's dependence on her are numerous. Let me quote one or two: "Who is rich? He whose wife's actions are comely. Who is happy? He whose wife is modest and gentle." Again: "A man's happiness is all of his wife's creation"; and yet again: "God's presence dwells in a pure and loving home." "Be not cruel or discourteous to your wife," said a first century teacher, "if you thrust her from you with your left hand, draw her back to you with your right hand." Another says: "A man should always be careful lest he vex his wife: for as her tears come easily, the vexation put upon her comes near to God." A seventeenth century writer states: "Never quarrel with your wife"; this is not to be done even "if she asks for too much money."

Such passages extend in an unbroken series through all

C. Gasquoine Hartley

medieval Jewish literature. But if the Jewish wife was held in honor by the Jewish husband, it was because of the very practical virtues of the Jewish way of living. The home life was everywhere serene and lovely, and if the Jew retained any virtue at all, he displayed it in the home. The father was the religious teacher of his family, and this duty necessarily increased his domesticity. He took greater interest in his children because it was his task to teach them the law, and his devotion to his wife was directly dependent on his service to the family. One of the Rabbis, on this question of the Jewish husband ill-treating his wife, said in framing his regulations "This is a thing not done in Israel."

I would ask you to note that the woman does not become a nonentity by reason of her limitation to a definite sphere of action within the home. Such a view is entirely absent among the Jews. The rule over the home-life held through the centuries by the Jewish wife is far more real in its results of power than the so-called equality claimed by a modern woman, acting under the influence of industrial ideals. What is significant (and ought to teach us if we can be taught) is the fact that such power is held by women in right of their position as wives and mothers; it is never extended to young girls or to unmarried women on account of their attraction and sexual power over men, in the way to which we have become accustomed. That is unknown, at least, in connection with marriage. The Jew understands that there are other ways of loving than falling in love. Power is held universally by the house mistress—the mother, whose desires through life are a law unto her husband and her children.

All Jewish literature is filled with examples of reverence expressed towards mothers who are "the teachers of all virtue." In the moral law the command to fear the mother—that is to treat her with respect, is placed even before the duty of fearing the father (Lev. xix. 8). Enduring evidence remains of the spiritual status of mothers. When the Prophet of Exiles wishes to depict God as the Comforter of his people, he says "As one whom his mother comforteth, so will I comfort you" (Is. lxvi. 13). When the Psalmist describes his utter woe, he laments, "As one mourning for his mother, I was bowed down with grief."

Perhaps, now as we see the mother taken as the one sufficient symbol of Jehovah's dealing with his people, the mourning for her presence being the completest expression of grief, we can come to understand something of the Jewish ideal of marriage and of the high honor, *because of this ideal*, in which women were held.

C. Gasquoine Hartley

VII

It should be plain enough now why English marriages so often are unhappy. The immense failure of marriage to-day arises from the confusion of our minds and our chaotic desires so that we have no firm ideal, no fixed standard of conduct either for the wife or for the husband. Every couple starts anew and alone, and the way is too difficult for solitary experiments.

The existence of many standards, of what ought to be done and what ought not to be done, the liberty permitted to the husband, the liberty permitted to the wife, if the wife shall continue her work or profession or remain at home dependent on the husband's earnings, whether the marriage shall be fruitful or sterile—these are but a few of the questions left undecided. And thus to leave unguided each wife and each husband, with their own idea of what is good to do and what is evil, makes for narrowness and waste of effort; while further, our inability to set up a standard of right and wrong conduct—of ideals to strive after—leaves vacant room for false ideals of every kind. These empty places of the mind have been occupied by the ravings of advanced people. The harm has been incredibly active in the consciousness of the young. We have put before their imagination nothing worthy of contemplation, therefore they easily sink downward attracted by what is base.

Then we suggest economic changes. But the evil is not economic. No evils are fundamentally economic. The structure of society is the unforeseen result of the conflicting desires and capacities of the individuals who comprise the society. A false view of marriage, a false view of the relative values of life and money, of service and liberty, of happiness and duty, is not dependent on economic conditions. Yet, let us not forget that this is the age of the gadding mind and the grabbing hand. We tend to value everything by what it brings in to us, in feelings if not in more tangible results.

You will see what this must mean. I am brought back to our wrong ideals; I have no new remedy to give; I can only again insist upon this truth: A preoccupation with a desire for love does not, and never can, result in happiness. But the personal (or perhaps my meaning will be clearer by saying the egoistic) view of love has assumed such gigantic proportion in our minds to-day that we accept these selfish desires as a safe basis for permanent happiness. *Marriage has ceased to be a discipline; it has become an experiment.*

The romantic view of love as the basis of marriage is, of course, the essence of the English habit of life; as we have seen, it focuses desire on personal adventures and personal needs. Romance necessarily leads to license, and not license of the body alone finding expression in more or less gross immoralities, for there is a spiritual license far more dangerous because so much more seductive. Appetite for adventure, for an excitement that is mainly mental is a condition that is quite as dangerous to marriage and much more common than the unfaithfulness that leads to the divorce courts.

I would appeal to the young, to each young girl, who to-day is questioning the future. Many of you have passed through a supremely heroic period of your lives; now you are waiting. You want to do right, and it is so difficult, for everyone seems to be at a loose end of desire. Perhaps some among you will ask me: "What can I do?" My answer is this: Fix your ideal. Do not make the child's mistake and think that the desirable thing is to do just what you like. You can never find freedom or happiness in that way. Hold firm in your hearts that no gain of personal liberty counts as happiness to

C. Gasquoine Hartley

women. Treasure your womanly qualities—your sweetness, your gentleness, your shyness, your unlimited capacity for devotion, guard these as your greatest possession. Do not acknowledge your poverty by failing to honor yourself. Be the establishers of a revived feminist idealism, the founders of a new tradition of womanly service. It is for you to fix the type that will one day give woman her real freedom; one day—but not yet.

In these times of uncertainty there is great danger. Every woman should be asked at the moment to believe in simple things; in her home, her children, her husband, and her country. The only hope is in unity, and for unity you must have discipline, and for discipline, for the present, at least, you must accept authority. Much, incalculably much, depends upon the young. The generation to which I belong is passing, we have to hand on to you who are younger the torch of life.

With more courage to face truth, you should have a surer ideal than we have found. When this comes, there will be less sentimentality but much deeper feeling about marriage. I have tried to show you a different ideal, and picture for you the Jewish home, where the exalted esteem in which women are held is the outcome of their attitude to marriage and the Jewish way of life: it is an ideal that depends directly upon duty and a religious view of marriage.

To-day we need a new consciousness of our social and racial responsibilities, the idea of handing down at least as much as we have received. Let the young women of England learn as a great new faith that the sons and daughters they bear are not their children and the children of their husbands only, but the sons and daughters of England—the inheritors of all the fine traditions of our race. Let us spread the new romance of Love's responsibility to Life; let us honor ideals of self-dedication to our husbands, understanding their dependence upon us, to our homes, to our sons and our daughters, to our race, its great ones and their deeds; our moral obligations to all children even before they are born.

It is women, and they alone, who can save marriage; they hold all life in their hands. Never before in the world has the opportunity been so vast; it is a fearful thing to find oneself among realities. To you, who to-day are young, negligence no longer is possible. Listen to what I tell you: those heroes who have died for this England of ours cry to you for children to hold their memories and make their lives everlasting.

Let us take seriously what the politicians have said without meaning it: let us make an England fit for heroes to be born in, able to mold a character of heroism in each of its children: not, as at present, an England so tainted with mean self-assertion that the dedication of a wife to her husband, of a mother to her children, counts as a sacrifice of her personality.[80:1]

FOOTNOTES:

[80:1] In order to guard myself from possible misunderstanding, I would wish to give the following explanation: the chief section of this essay on Marriage is devoted to praise of the Jewish ideal of marriage as a religious duty. It does not profess to examine the detailed working out of the ideal in connection with the definite regulations of traditional Judaism. That working out is, naturally, to the modern mind more or less faulty. It is as an ideal that I give it: an ideal of service and dedication that I want to be carried into English marriage, and to serve the needs of our national life. I would, however, make it clear that the detailed proposals put forward by me in the essays

C. Gasquoine Hartley

that follow have no connection with Judaism: no one of them could possibly be considered to have any such connection, except the proposal for facilitated divorce, but my proposal in that particular connection (as will be seen in the next essay) is hedged by restrictions, suggested by present-day circumstances.

THIRD ESSAY

THAT WHICH IS WANTING:

A CHAPTER WHICH ADVOCATES FREE DIVORCE

"That which is crooked cannot be made straight: and that which is wanting cannot be numbered."—Ecc. i. 15.

I

I am well aware that there will be many among my readers who, having gone so far in my book and agreed more or less with my point of view, must here fall into disagreement with me. This essay upholding free divorce, and the three that follow, the first one recommending regulation and firm action in suppressing prostitution as the only way to stay the spread of venereal diseases; the second essay on the illegitimately born child, where I differ in one important matter from the accepted view of what is chiefly needed to protect these unhappy children; and, even more, the proposal I make in the last essay, where I plead for an open recognition of honorable sexual partnerships outside of marriage—this half of my book will be disapproved of, very probably disliked, and my views more or less violently disputed. It will be said that what I advocate now is in direct opposition to my ideal of marriage being a religious duty, which demands the consecration of women to the service of the family and the home. This, however, is not so: if I have been understood at all, it should be evident that the opposition is not there.

I care little for our existing and chaotic forms of morality; what I desire is to create a new reality, the value of which consists in that it provides wider possibilities of decent and honorable conduct. We have to brave moral danger in trying to attain a higher moral reality. To me what seems the first necessity is to face things as they are, and not to go on eternally pretending that our world is what it is not.

Our vague-minded lax society has to pull itself together, has to reconsider and administer and formulate a more helpful system of regulations; has to learn to express again its united will in some better way than "go as you please," or fail. What is wanted is a new honesty to create standards of conduct, which will fix the every day indispensable duties, that, after all, make up the total of life. We have but a choice between the danger of falling deeper into confusion and dishonesty or the danger of awakening to a clearer and more difficult consciousness. Now, I do not believe it is moral to regulate life by fear, considering only the desire to remain undisturbed of those who are decayed and petrified. I do not know if I make my meaning clear. As our habit, we ignore or minimize all sex difficulties as much as we can; we hesitate and compromise and bungle over every reform because we are afraid of what may happen if we probe down to the real bottom of what needs to be done. We have neither the courage of our bodies or of our souls. This is why so often our attitude becomes false and our thoughts entangled, so that our moral life is corrupt with concealments and deceptions. Now, I am not content with the compromise which sanctions every form of sexual sin so long as the conventions are respected and the sin hidden—all the rottenness going on beneath the respectable structure of our society. I want as far as is possible to emancipate our lives from such slavery; to make less easy the hypocrisy which law and custom sanction; to gain freedom from a sham morality and the pretense of a righteousness that we do not maintain. It is a necessary step, for me at least, on the way to any kind of improvement. More and more I am convinced that we shall have to make a violent and very conscious effort to get clear of dishonesty.

That is why I am advocating, as a first most necessary reform, simpler and more decent facilities of divorce. I plead for a greater breadth of toleration, with a more honest facing of the facts, because I have known in my experience the degradation, the falsity and the absurdities that are going on to-day; the deceptions into which everyone is driven who is unfortunate enough to have to seek relief, under the present disgraceful divorce laws, from a marriage that has failed. There are conditions which degrade and embitter and make honorable conduct very difficult.

A great number of people, regarding marriage as a mystical and, therefore, unbreakable sacrament, object to divorce under any circumstances whatever. This is the case in Catholic countries, such, for instance, as Spain, the land I know and love so well. Such an attitude I can understand and respect, though I do not consider it a practical proposition, and know, moreover, that indissoluble marriage, in some ways, works very harmfully. It prevents hasty marriage. In Spain marriage is regarded as the gravest and most momentous step in life; but this caution does not altogether work out for good in the way one might expect.

I recall a conversation with a Spanish friend on this question.

C. Gasquoine Hartley

We were speaking of the great numbers of young Spaniards who did not marry. I asked my friend the reason of this. He answered: "You see we have no divorce in this land as you have in England, that makes us afraid now we have begun to think, we hesitate and hesitate, then we take a mistress while we are deciding, but it is easier and less binding to live like that, and we keep going on and put off marrying, sometimes put it off until it is too late." In Spain the illegitimate birth-rate is the highest of any country in Europe.

We must accept, then, that indissoluble marriage fails in practice, and the society which enforces it commits self-injury by setting up a standard of conduct impossible to maintain; and further, one that acts in deterring the more thoughtful from marriage and leaves the protected institution to the more reckless, who do not consider consequences.

Now, when once we do accept this, admit the principle of divorce and acknowledge that in certain circumstances the bond of marriage may be severed, at once the aspect of the question changes: it becomes a matter of practical adjustment, so that what is needed is decision and regulation of the conditions under which divorce should be allowed, so that they may meet best the needs of men and women in the society and, at the time, in which they live. I am very anxious to show the difference between the practical and the conventional attitude toward this problem. It is to be wished that this question of divorce could be approached free from the falseness of the old prejudices of religious intolerance and of sentimentality.

The great and pressing need of reform is being widely discussed at the present time. I note with a mixture of amazement and fear that practically in every argument the opinion universally held appears to be that the relief given should be as limited as possible; it is still being taken for granted that free divorce in this country is neither attainable nor desirable, and, indeed, that any extension of the grounds of divorce would act against the sanctity of marriage. I say I note this attitude with fear, because it seems to me that the triumph of prejudice and ignorance here is a most serious symptom of the degradation of our moral outlook and the poverty of our faith in the institution of marriage.

"Divorce is relief from misfortune, not a crime," to quote from the admirable statute book of Norway, a saying which should be one of universal application in divorce. And this relief must be granted, not merely as an act of justice to the individual; it is called for equally in the interests of society.

The moral code of any society ought to meet the needs of its members. But the needs change as time goes on, and moral codes must then also change or they become worn-out and useless. That society which is unwilling to modify its laws to fit new conditions drives its members into defiance of the law and acts directly as a cause of immorality. It were well to remember this as we come to question our laws of divorce. There can be no possible doubt that as the law stands at present it does not meet the needs of those people who claim its relief; while further, the most superficial knowledge of the situation proves how harmfully and immorally the law acts.

II

It is, of course, very much better that marriage should be as permanent as possible, and any society is obviously justified in bringing any moral pressure to bear to make people realize the seriousness of the relationship and the importance of keeping it permanent when possible. But it is certainly no part of the right or duty of society to use force to compel people to remain in the marriage relationship, when it becomes so repugnant to them that the conditions of the marriage cannot be continued. All that society has the right then to demand is that all the obligations which have been assumed shall be honorably fulfilled. But a relationship registered in mistake or under delusion should be subject to revision, and, with certain safeguards, to dissolution, otherwise the standard of morality is degraded and marriage itself is brought to contempt, and can be used, as indeed too often it is, as a cloak of protection for every kind of immorality.

But it is just here that the religious objector to divorce-reform steps in. Marriage, he declares, is not only a social institution, it is a sacrament of the Church, "Those whom God has joined together no man may put asunder," *therefore divorce must be made as difficult as possible.* As I have said before, I can respect the view that rejects divorce and regards the marriage bond as indissoluble, but I can have nothing but contempt for this attitude of weak and shuffling compromise. Much has been said on the matter, therefore I say little. I shall not attempt to urge the causes for which divorce should, or should not, be granted; for, as will appear directly, I want a much simpler and more radical reform: also I hold it folly to try to convince the self-blinded. I only ask the reader to make sure that he (or perhaps more probably she) really believes that the partners in the marriages that come to the divorce courts *were joined by God*, and is willing to follow the argument to its logical conclusion. Are they willing, for instance, to say that a woman or a man may not put aside the marriage if one of the two is a lunatic, or a hopeless drunkard, or an habitual criminal, or a degenerate, or the victim of a disease which can be communicated to the offspring? Are they willing to go with our ecclesiastical advisers, who seek to maintain marriages, which may be the cause of perpetuating disease and crime; the bringing into the world of the children of drunkards, of epileptics, of syphilitics and of lunatics?

Stop a moment and think what this must mean to the society in which we live. Can it be considered seriously that the continuance of marriage in such cases as these can by any juggling be made right—anything except the most blind-eyed folly and sin?

C. Gasquoine Hartley

III

Consider now the position to-day. Amazing marriages have been made under the urgency of war conditions, reckless marriages, entered into by those who have known each other for a few days only before marrying for life. A minister of religion stated quite recently, "I have had to marry many couples who admitted to me that they knew little about each other. I could do nothing. I was not allowed to refuse marriage."

There is no excuse now for these criminally hasty marriages; that they should have been made is one of the tragedies caused by war. It would prevent endless unhappiness and many divorces if marriages were to be made conditional, except under very special reasons, on the woman and the man having been engaged for a fixed and sufficiently long period. I would recommend this reform to all ecclesiastical opposers of divorce. Betrothal should be regarded as a much more important ceremony than is common with us: here again is a way in which we might wisely copy older civilizations, whose customs were more strictly planned to help men and women in right living.

In the first year of the war the number of cases heard in the divorce court rose from 289 to 520, which was the highest figure then on record. Last season the number had sprung up to 775, while on the present term's lists there are nearly 800 cases, showing the exceeding increase on the pre-war rate. A large percentage of the marriages which are dissolved by the court have been contracted since August, 1914. Petition after petition is filed praying for the dissolution of marriages which should never have been made. English law makes marriage far too easy. In addition to this alarming increase in divorce, a greater number of deeds of separation have been drawn up in the last two years than in any preceding twenty-five; cases of bigamy have also become very frequent, by women as well as by men.

A stage has now been reached when the cry for reform must be listened to. Something has got to be done. The unhappiness and failure in many marriages looms before us a colossal, an unprecedented and menacing fact. Our eyes cannot any longer remain shut to the damning proofs which confront us from so many sides.

IV

The question as to how our ridiculous and immoral system of divorce—(I really must use those terms)—was ever permitted to come into use may be answered very briefly. The Church ordained that marriage is indissoluble, but, this being found impossible in practice, the State stepped in with a way of escape—a kind of emergency exit. But what a makeshift it was! how flagrantly dishonest, how indecent! Adultery must be committed, and, in the case of the woman claiming relief, cruelty or desertion must be added to the adultery. To escape the degradation of an unworthy partner another partner must first be sought, home-life wrecked by the worst kind of conduct, and marriage degraded by an act of infidelity.

Now, this kind of thing is bad, and no possible shuffling can make it right; it is, indeed, so offensive to the feelings of most of us that it is very rarely, if ever, that the immoral and harmful way in which it acts is put into plain words.

The divorce law with its materialistic refusal to accept any grounds for divorce except physical infidelity, physical cruelty or desertion, makes for a low view of marriage. Further, it directly encourages perjury, in fact makes lying essential to obtaining the relief of the law. The law refuses to legalize divorce by the consenting desire of both parties—calls such a wise arrangement collusion; yet it cannot prevent what everyone knows is done in the great majority of decently conducted divorce suits, where desertion and infidelity take place by arrangement. The law is very lenient to those who can pay for the best arrangements for circumventing the law's intentions, but even in spite of the recent concessions, is still hard on the ignorant poor and low class. The law is a snob as well as a pedantic, pompous ass.

Some people may be disposed to believe that this very absurdity and unfairness of the law acts to prevent divorce. I tell you it does not; what it does do is to render decent and honest conduct quite impossible. I know this. I speak because the evil that is going on ought to be known. My own opposition to the law is not so much on account of the difficulty in obtaining a divorce—for it is not nearly so difficult as most people think; nor do I take exception, as is common with most women, to the unequal moral standard required from men and women; all this, as I have said, can easily be got over if you have money and a sufficiently clever lawyer. No, my passionate opposition is directed against the trickery and dishonesty made necessary by the law.

Let me prove this statement. To do so I will give brief details of four divorce suits which I think will speak more forcibly than any words of mine; in each case I know the facts I give are true.

Case 1.—A husband and wife, childless, desired to part, there was no physical infidelity on either side, but love had died. Both partners desired to remarry. The wife proved desertion against the husband (arranged between them beforehand by the help of a lawyer). She had to write and urgently entreat the man she desired to leave her to return! A decree for the restitution of conjugal rights was granted to her petition. Afterwards the husband had to commit adultery; (again arranged by the help of the lawyer.) He took the woman he wished to make his second wife for one night to an hotel. The decree nisi *was granted. Then there was the six months waiting for the decree to be made absolute. The King's Proctor made inquiries, it was found that the wife also desired her freedom; the divorce was refused on the ground of collusion. Four people were rendered desperately unhappy, compelled either to part or to live together without*

C. Gasquoine Hartley

marriage. This, as was to be expected, they did, and children were born, of necessity illegitimately.

Case 2.—In this case the husband loved his wife, but she had been unfaithful to him and desired freedom to re-marry her lover. There were no children. Because it was better for her, this wronged husband arranged for his wife to divorce him, prove desertion and adultery. There was a slight difficulty because it was the wife who had run away from home. However, this was easily got over. The wife wrote begging the husband to allow her to come home, representing that he had sent her away. He then had to reply refusing her request, and while desiring nothing on earth so much as her return to him, had to state he would never live with her again. An act of adultery was then necessary, and as this good and chivalrous husband was also an exceptionally moral man, he took his sister to an hotel, and the divorce was granted on this: they, of course, signing their names in the hotel register as Mr. and Mrs. X.

Case 3—In this case the action of the parties is reversed. The husband had committed adultery and wished his freedom to re-marry, but he held a public position, and to be the guilty party in a divorce suit meant social and financial ruin. The wife was innocent, and still loved her husband, but because she felt it right to free him, an act of adultery for her (not committed) was arranged. Both the decree nisi *and the decree absolute were granted. Complications arose from the fact that there were two children: as the "innocent" party custody was granted to the father, but he did not want the children. So for the six probationary months between the two decrees the children were placed with friends. Afterwards they were given back by the father to the mother.*

When the decree of a divorce has been made absolute, you can fortunately do what you like. During the six months probationary period, however, the "innocent" partner (see Case 1) has to be so careful of his or her conduct, that it is really much more convenient to be the "guilty" partner. I mention this as a further proof of the absurdity of the law, and the immoral way in which it acts.

Case 4.—This case was even more curious than the three I have given. A very bad but beautiful woman had married a man younger than herself, an idealist, chivalrous, and quite unusually moral. After a few years of hell the marriage had to be ended. In kindness, and because she was a woman, the man said she had better divorce him. Desertion was proved, though it had not taken place. Trouble arose from the necessary act of adultery, as it was against the principles of the husband even to appear to commit it. The difficulty had, however, to be got over or the divorce given up. It was done in this way: the man got his married sister to go with her husband to an hotel, personating him and a woman, and signing the hotel book with his name as Mr. and Mrs. —. Now the strange fact is that though there was no kind of similarity of appearance between the brother-in-law and the husband, one being very dark and the other very fair, one being short and the other tall, identity was established and sworn to by the servant in the hotel where the night had been spent. How this was arranged I do not know, but the decree nisi *and the decree absolute were granted without any difficulties arising.*

Now, none of these cases are unusual, with the possible exception of No. 4; similar divorce suits are heard each session, only that the way in which the details have been arranged is carefully hidden, to prevent the losing of the case on a charge of collusion. *The one absolute barrier in this land to the breaking of a marriage is that both parties want it to be broken.*

C. Gasquoine Hartley

It is obvious, surely, without any further argument, that laws making perjury necessary, which demand the committing of acts of, often pretended, infidelity, are immoral; nor is their immorality lessened by the fact that through the rather heavy costs of these "arranged suits,"[99:1] only the richer and more fortunate classes, as a rule, are able to bring them.

I ask if this state of things is to be allowed to go on: are decent people to be driven by the law to make use of such vile trickery? I say "decent people" advisedly, for those who bring this kind of suit *are decent*, wishing to act honorably and kindly, and carrying out the always difficult severing of the marriage bond with as little pain as possible. There are, I know, other divorce suits in which vindictiveness and jealousy and anger are the ruling motives, but undefended and "arranged" suits, more or less on the lines of those I have given, are becoming more and more frequent. Each law session their number is increasing. Personally, I regard this as an extraordinarily healthy sign.

V

I hope I have now sufficiently proved that our unclean divorce laws can do nothing to preserve the sanctity of marriage. If we know the facts, to go on pretending that we believe this is to mark ourselves as hypocrites. We need to get rid of a system that is as immoral in theory as it is evil in practice.

But, unfortunately, the probability of the law being reformed does not depend on the need for reform. How many people are affected? What votes will the advocating of the reform gain? Grievances that will not gather noisy crowds will continue unheeded. Modern parliaments are like badly brought up children; they can be bribed with promises of votes or frightened with fear of disorder, more easily than led by reason.

VI

As soon as we begin to consider the reform of the law, we come at once to such a tangle of questions that I have the greatest difficulty in finding the right end to unwind the skein. For the trouble with this matter of our divorce laws, as with most other reforms, is to decide just what ought to be done, how far are we prepared to go? where must the marriage bond be held tight? where may it be loosened? These are but examples of the questions that have to be answered. Hence the wrangling and the failure in establishing any kind of united will, which prevents anything at all being done. No one, for instance, can decide the causes for which it would be right to extend the grounds of divorce. Almost every individual interested, and every group of individuals, appears to have a different opinion and offers opposing suggestions. And the issues are further confused because any change that concerns marriage touches us all so intimately, so that the attitude that we take up must be strongly affected by our deepest emotions, which against our knowledge are directed by our unconscious wills. This explains much apparently unwise conduct, as well as persistent opposition to reform on the part of many humane people, that otherwise would be difficult to understand. There is much too great a timidity shown even by those who recognize most the evil done by our existing laws and work for their reform. They fear to ask too much, always the sure way to get nothing done.

This question of the causes for which divorce should be allowed is one that is very unlikely to be settled. I doubt if it can be settled wisely. In my opinion, an enlightened reform of our law must go much further than the providing of ways of escape from marriage. Such exits tend to destroy the happy working of marriage and open a direct way to abuses;

also they are unable to meet the needs of all classes, no matter how wide and numerous they are, while directly they are numerous they become ridiculous. They can never form the ultimate solution of what ought to be done. They tend to make marriage contemptible, and there are real grounds in the objections raised against them. There must be no special exits; the door of marriage must be left open to go out of as it is open to enter.

Nor do I believe there need be cause for fear in this idea of divorce by mutual consent. It is not nearly so easy to break a marriage that has lasted for any time as is usually thought by those who have never tried to do it. The habit of living together forges bonds you do not feel until you try to break them. The intimacy of marriage creates a thousand and one little every-day interests and ties, habits, preoccupations and memories in common; when they are torn it is like tearing thousands of little nerves that are far more painful than the one big hurt that caused them to be broken. That is why most marriages are dissolved through anger, in jealous passion, and because lovers are found out. It needs immense courage to sever a marriage if you have time to think what you are doing.

C. Gasquoine Hartley

About no subject, perhaps, are prejudices so rampant as they are about this question of changing the marriage laws. I am, however, very certain that I am right here. Nothing but good would follow from this introduction of plain simple honesty. There would be fewer divorces, and not more, if our laws were freed from their obsession with sexual offenses, and divorce was made a question of quiet and careful consideration, and mutual thought and decision.

There ought certainly to be a period of waiting after the application for divorce, which should be signed by both the partners of the marriage. I would suggest that the first application should be made to lapse of itself unless a further application for its enforcement was made after a period of— say, two years. Many people will go on with what they have begun, even if they don't want to do so, because they are not brave enough publicly to say they have made a mistake. After the second application a further period of waiting, not less than a year, might be required before the decree for dissolution of the marriage was made absolute.

I cannot understand how any honest mind can fail to see the advantages of this or some similar plan of divorce by mutual desire and arrangement, over the present law which forces the committal of perjury and requires adultery; nor can I find any reason why freedom should not be granted, when the marriage is childless and both partners, after sufficient deliberation, desire its dissolution. Probably it would be wiser, as a further necessary safeguard against too hasty parting, to require the marriage to have lasted for five years, before application for its dissolution could be made. I think, however, in urgent cases, and wherever it could be shown that the marriage had been entered into under a mistake and had been continuously unhappy, it should be possible to remit this requirement.

The case where one partner only of the marriage desires its dissolution is much more difficult, and cannot, I think, be settled with the same justice. I would, however, point out that the same situation is common before marriage, when an engagement is broken by one or other of the lovers, though, of course, the pain and injury (if such words can be used in this connection) must be much greater after marriage. The law allows in these cases compensation to be claimed by the injured partner for the harm suffered, and, though no one can uphold these breach of promise cases (which have increased so unfortunately in the war-period) it should be possible to avoid a similar sordidness. The establishment of right to compensation is not a new thing in divorce; used in the way I suggest it would serve as a safeguard against a too hasty escape from marriage, as well as being an act of justice for the partner who wished for the divorce to compensate, as fully as his or her means or working capacity permitted, the one who desired the continuance of the marriage.

The amount of compensation offered, as well as the amount claimed, if there was not an agreement between the partners, should be stated when application for the divorce is made; and this question should be settled before any further proceedings are allowed. The required periods of waiting would, of course, be enforced.

It may be interesting to my readers to learn that this principle of compensation, given by the partner who claims divorce to the one who does not desire it, is one that is common among many primitive peoples, especially wherever customs of maternal descent prevail.[106:1] It is practiced, to give one instance, by the Khasis, a maternal people of the hill tribes of East India; it affords an example of how much more wisely,

C. Gasquoine Hartley

because more simply, these matters are sometimes arranged, before civilization destroys our common sense.

VIII

So far, I have ignored the real difficulty of divorce—the child or children. At once the situation alters; when children are born both the practical needs and moral values are different. A marriage that becomes creative cannot be broken without grave disaster; for all creative things are eternal. What, then, must be done? Frankly, I know of no one workable plan, and I can suggest nothing except that in all cases the welfare of the children should be taken as the standard to which the desire of the parents should be subordinate.

You see, if we accept this standard of the child's good as the one thing of importance, we shall have great changes to make in our thought and in our action. I must follow this a little, though it takes me away from the main line of my argument, but I want to make quite plain the failure in our attitude. Perhaps on no other aspect of this question is greater nonsense talked than on this one of the effect of divorce on children. It is said so universally that it is better for the marriage to be broken than for children to live in a home in which the parents have ceased to love each other. I am not sure that this is true, the child's values are often very different from our adult values. Only just now I am reading "Joan and Peter," by Mr. Wells, and I am amazed at the levity with which he makes his characters treat this serious subject. You will remember the situation, almost at the opening of the book. Dolly, Peter's mother and the adopted-mother of Joan, has discovered that Arthur, her husband, has been unfaithful to their marriage. She is considering whether she will remain or will go to Africa with her cousin, Oswald Sydenham, who has for long loved her. These are the passages of which I wish to speak: "Then, least personal and selfish thought of all, was the question of Joan and Peter.

What would happen to them?" Dolly goes over the details of the situation, her certainty that Arthur would allow her the custody of the children, then the passage ends with this remarkable statement: *Oswald would be as good a father as Arthur. The children weighed on neither side.* A little later Oswald speaks on the same matter of the children's future. Dolly has asked him, "But what of Peter and Joan?" He answers, *Leave them to nurses for a year or so, and then bring them out to the sun.*

Now, to some people that sort of talk sounds all very well on paper, but as Mr. Wells and everyone ought to know, it is damnably different in practice. Shaw, Wells, Cannan, Beresford, and other writers have, in my opinion, done immense evil. They will present situations and treat them intellectually, without any honest facing of the facts. Children cannot be left for a few years and then picked up again like a bag or a trunk. The change of a father or a mother is a tremendous fact to a child, quite independent of whether the new parent is better or worse than the parent who has left. We know, as yet, very little of the results probable upon such a change, but we do know that confusion and jealousy are very likely to be stirred in the childish soul, and that these may work tremendous and lasting harm.

It has seemed worth while to bring this forward to show a little more clearly the complications which are set like a thick hedge around this problem. There is no easy way out, and the protection of the child's interests mean much more than provision for its bringing up and the satisfying of its physical needs. Only the parents who are sure that they are not claiming their individual right to freedom at the expense of the stronger home rights of their child or children can be held blameless in dissolving their marriage. We talk a great deal to-day about children and their welfare, but very few of us realize at all practically the change of attitude, the restrictions of the adult liberty and sacrifice that are likely to be necessary, if, under all circumstances, our theories are to be expressed in our daily conduct.

And this brings us straight back to the question we are considering at the very point at which we left it. For, if we place first the child's rights, we see at once that our existing divorce law does already in this matter fail, and fail very seriously.[110:1] A parent, either the father or the mother, may by neglect and many unkindnesses do far more injury to a child than by an act of unfaithfulness. I need not wait to prove this perfectly obvious fact. It seems to me, however, that these home-destroying acts, the result of any sort of daily indecency of living, which brings suffering, with lasting injury, to little children, are the one condition that makes divorce necessary and also right in a marriage where there are children.

I admit the difficulties of framing a law sufficiently elastic to meet this need. I do not, however, see that it would be impossible. The one who claimed the divorce—the father or the mother—or both if the dissolution of the marriage was desired by both parents, could be desired to state in the application for the divorce full answers to the following questions:—

(1) The reason or reasons on which the divorce was sought.

(2) The arrangements one or both parents propose to make for the after care of the child or children.

(3) The guarantees offered that these arrangements would be honorably fulfilled.

(4) Proof to be given by one or both parents that the continuance of the marriage would be harmful to the welfare

　　　　C. Gasquoine Hartley

of the children.

Perhaps you will object that such a law would limit too much the liberty of the parents. I acknowledge this, and I think such limitation is right. You see, I do not believe in the kind of liberty that makes it easy for anyone to do wrong to helpless children.

Science has now shown us how terribly the future of the child depends on its early relationships in the home: its relation to its mother, its relation to its father, to its brothers and sisters. These early home relationships assume a much deeper aspect, and are, indeed, the most important influence in the life of every human being. Parenthood is far more nearly eternal than we knew. It is this tremendous fact, from which there can be no kind of escape, that ought to decide our attitude and direct us in framing an honest and clean divorce law. This protection of those who cannot protect themselves is the one essential and right consideration. The law must take action to guard all children that the failure or folly of their parents do not fall too heavily upon them.

There is little more that I need to say. A hard and fast divorce law cannot, I am sure, meet the needs of the young people of the new generation; moreover, it cannot but act to degrade marriage. Marriage is too difficult—the needs of children, as well as the needs of men and women are too complicated for the old standards of punishments. Divorce as it exists at present is a revenge, it ought to be a help to honorable conduct; it depends now upon a committal of perjury and adultery, it ought to depend on honesty and on a right fulfilling of responsibilities.

FOOTNOTES:

[99:1] Since writing this essay the admirably courageous and honest letter of Commander Josiah Wedgewood has appeared, in which he gives the details of his own divorce suit.

[106:1] See for other examples "The Position of Women in Primitive Society."

[110:1] In this connection see the admirable essay on Divorce by Mr. H. G. Wells, in "An Englishman Looks at the World."

FOURTH ESSAY

"GIVE, GIVE!"

SOME REMARKS ON PROSTITUTION, AND AN INQUIRY AS TO THE BEST MEANS OF PREVENTING THE SPREAD OF VENEREAL DISEASES.

"The horse-leach hath two daughters, crying, Give, Give!"—Pro. xxx. 15.

I

Many observers point out an increase in loose conduct during the war. In that period there were established large camps of soldiers in lonely places, who were freed from the neighbor's eye: women also were withdrawn in large numbers from the influences of the home. The war lessened restraints and increased temptation.

I will refer to two out of many newspaper cuttings which dwell on the consequent evils:—

WOMEN, WAR, AND MORALS

Mr. Justice Darling's View

Mr. Justice Darling, in a case at the Old Bailey yesterday, said the harm the war had done to the morals of the people of this country was far beyond the material damage.

In nothing had it done more harm than in the relaxation on the part of the women of this country. This had now reached a point that it could be seen in a walk along the street. Women differed by the width of Heaven from what their mothers were.

This is quite the hardest thing that has been said about women, the hardest comparison that could be made; but unhappily it cannot he denied. And a second paragraph, taken from the *Daily Telegraph*, carries us a stage further, from cause to effect. The looseness of morals has increased alarmingly the spread of venereal diseases.

"Giving evidence before the National Birth Rate Commission in London, Dr. E. B. Turner, after advocating early marriage and urging the necessity for a higher moral standard, without which venereal diseases would never be kept down, made this statement:

"These diseases were now being spread not only by professional prostitutes. People had gone wrong through the wave of sentimental patriotism which had swept over the country. Out of 112 soldiers taken to the Rochester Road Institution, only fourteen had contracted disease from professionals. The others had contracted it from flappers."

The condition of the streets is such that it is not safe to let any young man or boy walk about, not so much because of

C. Gasquoine Hartley

prostitutes, men may learn to avoid them, but because of dressed-up, flighty girls, who have earned big wages during the past four years, and now are feeling the want of money to spend upon dress and pleasure. Almost for the first time girls have had money, and it has enabled them to do what they want; they have learned more than their mothers know and, therefore, they despise their mothers' ideas of what is fitting and natural. Modern girls are out to get all they can, and by any means. It is, I know, easy to exaggerate the situation. I have, however, taken pains to gain all possible information on the subject. I find it the opinion of those who are best qualified to know that the most alarming feature of the problem now is the greatly increased danger of spreading the diseases, caused by the shifting of infection from the professional prostitute to young girls out for larks and presents. I was told by one worker in the Police Court Mission, for instance, of a club for girls, aged from fourteen to twenty-six years, among whom *there was probably not a single pure girl*. A woman rescue worker said that "South London was swamped by these larking girls," so many cases come up that "no one knows what to do with them." In the Police courts, while the number of women charged had lessened considerably, the number of girls charged has increased three-fold. Many of these girls are very young; some of them hardly more than children. In almost all cases the charge made is the same—disorderly conduct with soldiers. Of the number of girls convicted and sent to prison or to rescue homes, *at least three parts are found to be infected*, the greater number with gonorrhoea, but some with syphilis.

Now, it is no part of my purpose to blame women. The great majority of these girls are ill-trained, and have been worked beyond care for decency. The question is, what it is best to do. The answer is not easy. For while everyone is agreed about the need for action, disagreement as to what form the action shall take hinders the adoption of any wider course of prevention. Here again there is no unity of purpose, no humility to accept what is right.

C. Gasquoine Hartley

II

For myself, I shall try to avoid a purely moral and idealistic treatment of the subject. At the same time, before explaining what practical measures should, in my opinion, be taken to lessen the evils, I should like to refer briefly, and I know inadequately, to the deeper causes, which are rooted in our attitude of life, as well as dependent on our hidden desires. Man, and of course I include woman, as a whole is estimated at too low a value. It is a paradoxical consequence that the *parts of man*, I mean his separate organs, rise in value. His brain, his sex, his stomach—each strives for mastery in attention; a faithless age has manias of sexuality, of intellect, of gastronomy.[117:1] These manias are the result of low values really placed on man himself. How do we discover that low value? It is not so much a matter of opinion; far more important than the opinion of the public is the widespread, always-acting, fundamental public feeling, expressed in the atmosphere of our society. Every smallest detail of life, our aims and hourly habits, everything that makes up the secret imaginations and the un-willed purposes of life—all have a part to play in deciding what our estimations of life will be, the things we shall seek as desirable, what avoid as unpleasant. If our estimations and hidden desires in actual fact rise in goodness, if we find better aims to satisfy our lives than the excitements of sexual satisfaction, then this department of morality will rise.

The question is one of great complexity, and the surest means of improvement are very difficult to decide; not to be settled in a spirit of Sunday-school optimism. The bad boy does not always come to harm, or the good boy gain the reward that he ought to have. It is not so simple as that. Even if all vulgar and evil desires could by some magician's wand be transformed into their opposites, so that all of us bubbled and seethed with virtues, I do not believe we could count on the results. Our very virtues might hasten us to perdition: both higher and lower aims, if ill-adjusted to form a complete life, may lead astray. The savage in us all has to be reckoned with as the angel, and the dreamer who ever looks to heaven often stumbles over a tiny stone. Thus a helpless romanticizing, a too ideal as well as a too low view of love, may lead easily to a self-deceiving resort to prostitution.

All forcing of goodness, in my opinion, is dangerous. Often the cause of virtue is injured, like the cause of religion, not only when virtue is allied with routine, dullness and narrowness, but also when appeal is made to aspirations, which the young rarely feel spontaneously, aspirations ill-adapted and too high for their immature characters and the needs at the stage of virtue that has been reached. Certainly they *appear* to respond, fall in with our plans of salvation and often accept them with seeming joy; I venture, however, to think that very often this external attitude does not in any way correspond with the internal one, that very often there has been disturbance and shock, to be followed later by increased need for excitement, with an impulse to more perilous adventure to cover the unconscious feeling of frustration and disappointment; while another result is a sense of unreality, a state always unfavorable to moral health.

If morality is seen as something overbeautiful for daily use, even more than as something dull, inactive, over-prudent; if vice, on the other hand, is conceived as easy, brilliant, gay, gallantly reckless, in opposition to the too ethereal or merely stupid and prosaic aspects of life (though in reality seldom do the dissipated and those who prey on the vices of mankind possess any brilliance or originality), then beauty and virtue will aid vice, through the stimulus of contradiction it will provide. Vice will gain by the brilliance, wit and

C. Gasquoine Hartley

beauty, which the artists and creators of the world ought to be induced, were the world's cause properly cared for, to connect with virtue.

The popular view of our common motives still inclines to reduce everything to a single impulse—the young are moved exclusively by self-interest and the search for pleasure. But surely this view is false. Hazlitt, the English essayist most interested in psychology, in his essay on "Mind and Motive," correctly observes that, "love of strong excitement both in thought and action" has much more influence on our ideas, passions and pursuits than mere desire for the agreeable. Curiosity itself, also the love of truth, "our teasing ourselves to recollect the names of persons and places we have forgotten, the love of riddles and of abstruse philosophy," he holds these to be illustrations of "the love of intellectual excitement," and, with respect to this curiosity, he holds that our vices are more due to it than to sexual gratifications, saying with regard to vicious habits, "curiosity makes more votaries than inclination."

We find, then, that the difficult problem we are considering, like other social problems, has a material aspect, that is a medical aspect, an intellectual aspect, and a spiritual aspect concerning the aims of life: and of these the last is the most fundamental; it is obviously also the most difficult. To attack the situation fully it would be necessary to change most of our contemporary life. We are, however, bound to realize that, if we are to succeed, our attention must shift from saving the fallen, to removing the hindrances and the temptations that are the causes of falling. In other words, we have to provide a society in which the young will find virtue and goodness as serviceable to their needs and as attractive as vice and doing evil.

III

If we turn now to the practical consideration of the problem before us, we find the situation, difficult as it is, is not without hope. We have to face as the result of the war a task greatly enlarged and growing in difficulties, but if we do so face it—and the very increase in the danger is urging us like spurs in the flesh of a tired horse—we have an exceptionally favorable opportunity for correction and amendment. For one thing, we have become more used to being interfered with, also, I think we have come to understand in a new and more profound way that each man "is his brother's keeper." Again the real difficulty arises now, not so much from our want of good will, as from our failure to act unitedly, and formulate and carry out a wide-reaching program of reform.

If for the sake of clarity, we try by classifying motives to form a rough grouping, we find that, as with most political subjects, there are three opinions with regard to proposals for State interference to stay the peril and prevent the spread of venereal disease.

The first school favors extreme State interference. Persons suspected of disseminating disease (or "denounced by one of the opposite sex" as having done so) are liable to be arrested, medically examined, and, if necessary, detained for re-examination and for treatment until cured: habitual prostitutes can be sentenced to imprisonment. Possibly State-inspected brothels will be established; all street solicitation treated as an offense. Compulsory medical certificates of freedom from infectious venereal diseases will be made a legal prerequisite of marriage; all wishing to be married, when found infected, to be registered and treated until certified free from infection. State provision of hygienic preventative and curative means are to be given free to those

C. Gasquoine Hartley

in danger from infection as well as to all suffering from venereal diseases. Finally, severe police action is urged against agents, landlords, publicans, restaurant and hotel-keepers, theater, music-hall and cinema owners, fortune-tellers—and everyone directly or indirectly profiteering by prostitution. This is not a description of any one national treatment, or proposed treatment of the problem, but rather a composite hotch-potch, intended to include the main features of the new and old schemes based on State interference and regulation of vice.

The opposite school of thought produces an opposite scheme; one that I may, perhaps, call an ethical Sunday-school plan of salvation by means of guidance and gentle persuasions. They would educate people in the fact that all *promiscuous intercourse is likely to be dangerous*, and recommend only an alteration of the laws of marriage and divorce to meet cases of marital infection and to protect children who are infected by negligence. Such a course of mild action is widely supported by bishops and by "sheltered" women, who reveal to us curiously the psychology of the class, which, throughout the Victorian period, practiced idealism on the easiest methods.

The practical objections usually advanced to "the inter-ference school" are that laws of regulation create an illusory sense of security which encourages vice and increases the spread of disease. No inspection, however widely and well regulated, can guarantee that it will detect *all* infected persons, but the idea will prevail that all infected at any time are "locked up." A still stronger objection as urged by women, arises from the fact that the law will not be equal in its treatment of the two sexes: the man on the spree after his day's work will seek his pleasure without danger of the law's hand, while a woman, *in a similar position, in work and not asking for money*, will be liable to arrest for soliciting, and detention and imprisonment, if affected. I shall have more to say soon on this question; here I will remark only that in bringing forward these objections I am not stating opinions of my own, but trying to be fair to objections, which, I know, are strong in the minds of the majority of women. But I diverge a little in these comments from my present work of classifying schemes.

The third type of treatment pursues, of course, a moderate, middle course. Registration and treatment of disease should not be compulsory, because, as opinion at present is, this course will lead merely to concealment on the part of the sufferers, whereas medical treatment at the earliest possible hour is what is aimed at; but free treatment and provision of curative safeguards should be provided to all who apply for them, and always with secrecy. (There is much opposing opinion as to which of these two preventative plans— providing of disinfectants to be used *before* or of remedies to be used *as soon as possible after the act*—is the more effective.) No wide-spread schemes for examination and detention are recommended, rather are they discouraged; nor is there any firm regulation for ending street soliciting. Certificates of health should *not* be made a legal pre-requisite to marriage, but the existence of venereal disease should *annul* marriage without expense, making the law applicable to the poor as well as to the rich. Also, medical men should be specially authorized, without risk of libel, slander or other legal attack, to inform parents or guardians or others directly interested, that anyone contemplating marriage, a man or a woman—is in an infectious state.

It may be pointed out here that military authorities seem to lay stress on one thing that some people will say has nothing to do with the subject—the provision of proper means of recreation. Personally, I would emphasize this aspect of the question to which I have but just now referred. If the

C. Gasquoine Hartley

amusement is to fulfill the purpose required, and be really a strong counter attraction from vice, it must be the kind of recreation desired and liked by the young people for whom it is provided, not merely the recreation that is considered good for them by the adults who provide it. This opens up, of course, a whole welter of questions. I am not advocating bad and low class entertainments; I hate them and think their suggestive influence a curse among us. Yet, I do fear the adverse action of any kind of amusement that takes the form of an unliked and moral-forcing hot-house.

The fluttering about, the glitter and glare of dissipation, is always, I think, at first the fierce striving of a sickly life towards the only attractive and visible light. Certainly the providing of wholesome amusement is necessary, but, in relation to all the change that is really called for, this is just about as important as the giving of packets of sweets. What is wanted is a wiser understanding of the many and conflicting needs of the young; the provision of the opportunities and outlets which their bodies' and souls' growth demand; needs which must be gratified, or the body, driven by dissatisfaction and curiosity, seeks the gratification that has been taken away from the creative soul.

IV

But to return to plans of action for fighting this scourge. The fight has to be made, and to be begun at once. It is stated that there were, at the beginning of the year, in the neighborhood of 20,000 infected men receiving treatment in our Army and Navy Hospitals. According to the estimate of the Royal Commission on Venereal Diseases published in 1916 there were, at that time, something like 3,000,000 syphilitic persons in the Kingdom, 450,000 in London alone. Since 1916 the number must have greatly increased. Many diseases are more immediately fatal to mankind than are these diseases, but none are so disastrous in their effects. To take but two examples of their destructive incidence; it is known that to them more than half of both the blindness and the lunacy in this country is directly due. But I need not trouble you with facts and figures that to-day are known to almost everyone.

What is needed now is a world-wide, organized plan of defense, modified possibly to meet the special requirements of different countries, but, as far as is possible, the same for the whole world. A first step has been taken, at the meeting of the Red Cross Societies of the world, which was held at Cannes, in April, 1919. No man can tell how far-reaching its work will prove: an International Health Bureau was instituted and arrangements made for a further great conference to be held at Geneva after the signing of peace.

I would like to wait and write of the Cannes Conference, which to me was an event more serious even than the other world conference, where some were thoughtlessly and selfishly juggling with human affairs. Here was no pretending, no hiding of motives, just a facing of the real situation. The great events of life are almost always quiet. I picture the

C. Gasquoine Hartley

great ball-room,[129:1] where usually jazzes and one-steps were indulged in by the officers of the Allied Armies and bright girl W.A.A.C.S. and W.R.E.N.S., occupied now with grave men; a group of some of the greatest scientists ever assembled together. United they seek for the first time how best an end may be made to this tragic scourge of our civilization;[129:2] their fervent purpose should light a flame to blaze in action in every civilized country.

It would be impossible to over-emphasize the importance of the findings of this Conference. We women are glad to know that the Committee reported unanimously against State regulation of vice and State toleration of prostitution. At the same time, the repression of all street-soliciting was advocated, as well as control of restaurants, hotels or other places with reference to their use for promoting prostitution. The Committee further favored the detention and, where necessary, the isolation of all persons known to be, or suspected of being infected, and advocated the adoption of the report system in regard to early preventive treatment. The importance of early marriage was urged. Other measures recommended were the custodial care of the feeble-minded, and State control of the use of alcohol.

So many people, and especially, I think, women are led astray by sex sentiment as soon as they approach these problems. I do not believe that this can be avoided, but we may guard against it. Thus, those who hesitate, and there are many who do hesitate, in adopting the proposals of the Cannes Committee, which are aimed, either directly or indirectly, against prostitutes, should take care to consider all the facts. Of late there has been exhibited in this country a rather bewildering sentimentality about this matter. The experience of the American Army authorities should teach us a much-needed lesson. The American program to maintain the sexual health of the men went much further than any

English proposal, straight and without sentiment to the main cause of the disease, in a way that should shame our vacillating methods.

"The repression of prostitution was declared to be a public health measure, and all public health departments were required to cooeperate actively with the proper law authorities in minimizing its practice." When the American armies entered France, the same end, of keeping the men from "coming in contact with the prostitutes, either public or clandestine," was always kept in view. The difficulties were immense. At that time (from August to the early part of November, 1917) the troops were stationed in certain French towns, where the houses of prostitution were running wide open and were frequented by large numbers of men. On November 15th all these houses were placed out of bounds. The table on the following page shows what happened.

Month	No.of Troops.	No.of Prophylaxis.	Disease Cases.	Rate p. 1000.
Houses open.				
August	4,571	1,669	72	16
September	9,471	3,392	124	13
October	3,966	2,074	67	16
Houses out of bounds.				
November	7,017	885	81	10
December	4,281	539	44	10
January	3,777	523	8	2

Take also these figures: in one body of 7,401 troops belonging to various branches of the service, with an average of seven weeks in France, only 56 prophylactic treatments were given, and only one case of venereal disease developed; again, during two months in France, one infantry regiment of 3,267 men had a record of only eleven prophylactic treatments, and no case of disease. But perhaps the most

C. Gasquoine Hartley

effective example of the efforts made by the American authorities to repress prostitution in France occurred at Blois. American troops arrived at the town in January, 1918. The brothels were at once placed out of bounds, but, shortly afterward, and, owing to protestations on the part of the French authorities,[132:1] the order was relaxed, in so far as one of the brothels was taken over for the use of the American soldiers. Not for long was this tolerated. On March 21, this brothel also was put out of bounds. Strict repressive measures against prostitution and street-walking were put in force; and repeated arrests—by the military police—both of prostitutes and suspected prostitutes, succeeded in almost ridding the town of this menace.

The result was very interesting. I will quote directly from the article from which these facts are taken:

Although politicians and the owners of cafes and brothels continued to protest, the decent elements of the community gradually changed from an attitude of skepticism, even of hostility and resentment, to one of appreciation, commendation and cooeperation. An official report from the Surgeon-General's office on conditions in the town declared:

"It is evident that placing the houses at Blois out of bounds has had a wonderful effect, not only in lowering the venereal rate, but in improving the morality of the soldiers and also of the civil population."

Of course, these few figures and scattered facts cannot tell the whole story; they do, however, indicate with sufficient clearness what may be done by firm and fearless action.

V

Let me try to make the position clearer by means of another and quite different illustration. The results of restrictions on the drink trade in England during the war showed that legislative interference with strict rules can do much more than many of us believed.[134:1] Wipe off all that is doubtful in the results, all evasions of the law, all that was due to the absence of a large number of healthy men, yet the State interference—prohibition of treating, great shortening of hours, provision of weakened beer—these undoubtedly have acted so as to reduce drunkenness.

Surely this must serve as a great proof that the removal of temptation is the one effective remedy to help men and women and to prevent sin. A man who got into trouble with a woman not very long ago, gave as a defense in police court: "You can say 'No' to one woman, but when they are round you all the time you can't."

The three objections specially urged by women against laws directed against prostitution and prohibiting solicitation are:—

(1) That such laws cannot prevent all solicitation. This may be granted, but it does not prove that they may not greatly lessen the evil of solicitation. It may be granted, in the same way, that no State prohibition can prevent all secret drinking. But this is no reason for or against prohibition; the question is what it does do, not what it does not do.

(2) That such laws act unequally for the two sexes,—that is, that a man is never, or almost never, made specially liable for soliciting and worrying women. This objection is really quite absurd, and it is only on account of the frequency with

C. Gasquoine Hartley

which it is urged by women that I refer to it again. For the life of me, I cannot see how any woman reconciles it with her conscience to bring forward such a silly evasion. A woman can always give a man in charge who annoys and insults her; moreover, in the vast majority of cases she could without effort protect herself from any such annoyance. Laughter is a weapon that will dishearten the most persistent man-follower. Besides, as every one of us knows, solicitation is the woman's act, and not the man's in ninety-nine out of a hundred of these cases. The man may be ready, possibly he may seek, but he seeks only where he knows the one sought will invite. This objection cannot then, in honesty, stand.

(3) That such laws encourage blackmailing by the police; also that the police may arrest poor, hard-working and defenseless girls, out for a legitimate lark and charge them by error or vindictively. The fear of blackmailing by the police is, I think, the one valid objection. Possibly it can be met by a much wider use of women police; the second objection of the poor defenseless girl, wrongly charged, leaves me quite unmoved. Again the remedy is in the girl's own hands. But, as a matter of fact, the police are so afraid of making a mistake that, almost in every case where there is a doubt, they do not charge.

Those—again I must add especially women—opposed to State interference in these matters must ask themselves on what grounds their opposition is based: should we not consider the health of society in the present and the future well-being of the race as more important than our personal distaste and intellectual dislike of interference? Even *liberty* must not take up a disproportionate amount of space in our view. My own belief in the efficacy of making right doing as simple as is possible by lessening temptation, is based on what life has taught me, that the fundamental character of people is not greatly alterable, but that the alteration of their circumstances will certainly influence the effect and working of their capacities and instincts. The buttercup which is tall with a flower at the end of a high firm stalk and leaves with slender spike fingers, if it grows in an open meadow, becomes a stunted flower on a short stem, and its leaves form squat webs, in order to force its growth on a close-cropped lawn. The experience of the American Army shows us that to cut off opportunity and suggestion of temptation, the incentives to libidinous imagination, is to alter character more than everyone recognizes. When I think of this achievement, gained in so short a time and with so simple means, I confess I lose patience with the opposition raised by the women of this country against every attempt at legislative interference with prostitution. Nothing can be done thoroughly because of this hindering folly. There really is no limit to women's sentimental egoism and their blindness in turning from facts.

We pray in our churches "lead us not into temptation," but we leave our streets crowded with temptations. Surely this is stupid negligence and worse. Remove the temptations, and as a nation we shall be delivered from evil.

C. Gasquoine Hartley

VI

Now, a friend who has read this chapter up to this point, objects that I am laying too great stress on one aspect of the problem, bringing forward with undue insistence the importance of restricting prostitution—the removal of the woman tempter as the only practical way to prevent the spread of sexual diseases. She does not, I think, like my dismissal of conscious moral striving from a principal place in my scheme of reformation. That, at least, I gather from what she has said to me. Stronger, however, than this feeling, is, I am sure, an unconscious, or at any rate an unacknowledged, irritation at what she feels to be a failure on my part *to blame men*; I say too little about their weakness and their lust.

I grant this. In the first place I am convinced of the folly of preaching to anyone. Then, as I am always asserting, I believe in the continuous responsibility of woman, and, therefore, if I am to be honest, I must accept here as in all relations between the sexes, the validity of the man's plea that rings—yes, and will continue to ring—through the centuries: "The woman tempted me." We are dealing with forces that I do not believe can be set aside, forces active long before human relations were established, which press on women back and back through the ages. Woman possesses the sacred right of protecting man, it is a duty imposed upon her by nature, and one that she cannot safely escape. Let me assert that this is no sentimental statement. The essential fact in every relationship of the sexes is the woman's power over the man, and it is the misuse of that power that leads to all prostitution.

VII

I want now, in a final section of this chapter, to consider, as fully as the limits of my space will allow, the outside facts of prostitution—that is, the popular view on the subject.

Externally, prostitution exhibits two factors: lust in men and a dependent condition among women, which makes them surrender themselves as victims to this lust. This is the accepted, sentimental, and picturesque description: a sort of compound of sinfulness and pathos, making a draught, if the truth is faced, not always altogether unpleasing to women, a fact which surely accounts for the excitement and veiled pleasurable curiosity with which the subject usually is approached. For the lust, men are held responsible, and the chaste characters of women are held up in contrast. Now, it is this view of the matter which affords prostitution one of its most certain opportunities of permanency: also it gives women, when they attack it, all the pleasing satisfaction of virtue that is realized without effort. At the same time, it explains why they object to repressive measures that are framed to end it.

During the agitation, for instance, for the repeal of the 40 D Act, women and women-like men wallowed in right-eousness. Never did I hear more nonsense talked than at the meetings I attended on this subject. Women's instinctive attitude had a unique chance of displaying itself, and one wondered at the combined prudery and sentiment with which the subject was approached, while the most offensive part of their conventionalism was the sex-obsession, which was clotted, like cream turned sour, on all their judgments.

Consider again the controversy that has raged with regard to the providing of prophylactic outfits to our men in the Army and Navy. One would think this was a simple matter. Precautions taken before, or within a short time after contact, enormously lessen the dangers of infection.[141:1] And yet prophylaxis is objected to on the grounds that it is immoral: that it invites to sexual indulgence by providing immunity from infection. It is also held to give rise to a false security.

Really, it is difficult to have patience. Huge sums are being spent in treating these diseases after they have been contracted, but we must not give our young men the means whereby they may be prevented from being contracted. Such miserable prejudice would be funny, unless one remembers the unconscious cause which gives it so burning a strength.

Some months ago, during the war, I attended a conference to protest against the giving of prophylactic outfits to the overseas troops. It was called and conducted by ladies, the incarnation of all the virtues, effervescing in the most appalling sentimentality I have ever come across, even at meetings of women met to discuss the morals of men. Interminable floods of gush! They talked of nothing but purity, its beauty, its healthfulness, its moral uplifting to the soul of the young man—its Devil knows what. Venereal diseases were nature's punishment for impurity; to provide prophylaxis was to insult the pure youth, to hurry on to sin the youth who was not pure. Such was the pleasing doctrine slowly and solidly defended, while the real problem of how to prevent the spread of venereal diseases—especially how to stop the birth of infected children, was lost in white clouds of virtue. And many of these women themselves were mothers! When I remonstrated, attempted to show that the one fact to go for was the prevention of infection as in that way only could the spread of the plague be stayed and the innocent saved from suffering with the sinner, I was charged, denounced, and cut to pieces. I am sure that every one of those good women pitied me—as a matter of fact, one speaker said frankly that she was very sorry for my son; plainly they were very doubtful of my virtue. Since that day I have noted that very few invitations to attend Women's Conferences have been sent to me.

This shelving of the real facts, of course, is unconscious on the part of women. The lust of men as the true cause of evil is the one popular and accepted view of the situation, and from this it follows that the prostitute is the man's victim, and as such must be protected. This is highly pleasing; a view depending, as it does, on the moral superiority of women, which stands them as Amazons of purity on the glorious mountain heights of virtue, from where they must send down climbing ropes and ladders, in the form of moral warnings and carefully edited sexual instruction, possibly made pleasing by cinemas and theater illustrations, to pull men up out of the deep valleys of vice.

Yet this view is singularly untrue; for if we inquire into this question of men's lust, it is obvious that not they, but women, are the more responsible. How often it is woman who awakens this male lust, fans it to flame, feeds it to keep it at fever heat. Woman indeed must so act, since nature urges behind; but the prostitute uses this power without rest, she lives, not indeed sacrificed by men's lust, but kept alive by it. Always there is the invitation—"Come and find me." To be provocative is the one fixed simple rule of her life. Men's lust is a necessity to her very existence. Starving nations do not so eagerly await the coming of the food-laden ships which will keep them alive as the prostitute watches for the rising of the male desire. The dismay when it is reluctant to quicken is as sincere as it is disquieting to acknowledge. In the final result the woman may be the victim, but at the start she is the controller of the assault. She directs a continuous attack; her relation to men is comparable to that of a magnet to a heap of iron filings.

C. Gasquoine Hartley

Most men, it is true, are not only tolerant of women's wiles; they like them. But most men succumb, I believe, against their will, and often against their inclination to this tyranny of lust. Men's chivalry as well as their pride has woven a cloak of silence around this question; this silence has protected women—even the worst.

There is such a thing as too much temptation for a man; temptation that a woman has no right to give unless she knows a man loves her and is ready to marry her. It is damnably hard on men.

The truth in these matters is not often spoken. In spite of the emancipation upon which they pride themselves, in spite even of much precocious experience, almost all women lead a shielded life; vast tracts of experience are usually outside their knowledge or their power of comprehension. This explains, I think, their belief in the old fiction that the seduction of men by women does not take place, but all men know it goes on unceasingly. Women have been shielded by men to an extent which few of them acknowledge. This is one reason why the best of them find it so difficult now to face the woman's responsibility in these problems of sex frankly and simply.

At one time this failure in feminine honesty on the part of so many advanced women made me angry as it appeared to me to be a conscious shirking. I know now I was wrong; this attitude is an unconscious one and this makes it much more dangerous. I fear nothing can change it, at least, for a very long time. As women's spiritual temperature rises, their honesty tends to fall, so much sometimes as to freeze their intelligence.

Women, even the fairest and most advanced, are willing to accept little shame for a depravity which their sex shares equally with the inescapable and surrendering enemy—man. Perhaps the position is unavoidable. I am not certain, and it is very difficult to find the truth. But no man, I think, could satisfy completely in woman the craving for dominion, which the delusive humility of his desire awakens. Then when a woman commits the error—from a womanly point of view—of hunting down her man in haste for gain, instead of drawing and binding him slowly and unconsciously by love, she awakens the same instinct for dominion in the man. It is the lust to devour, to crush, quickened into being by suggestion. It explains, perhaps, the cruelty of all wild-love.

The position now in relation to the problem we are considering, and keeping in view these facts of the relationship of the woman and the man, should be clearer: the spread of venereal disease must be attacked by restricting the trade of the prostitute. Action must begin there. Acknowledging frankly women's power over men and the magnitude of the temptation they exercise, we must accept the best means to control it. America has proved what can be done. We want strong restrictive laws to prevent street soliciting and make possible the detention of every infected person.

Why can't we face the situation now when we are trying to tidy up our social life. Health, that was necessary in war time, is surely equally important in peace? Even the prostitute, the professional and the amateur, will benefit: restrict the opportunities of this easy way of getting money and presents from men and other ways of living and obtaining presents must be resorted to. Thus there will be a finer chance of reformation than ever there was before. To urge moral reforms, to talk sloppy nonsense about liberty, about the poor prostitute, police interference, and all that humbug; to seek cover under "the unequal action of the laws between men and women," or any other form of excuse, is willfully to falsify the position. For myself, I assert without a

C. Gasquoine Hartley

shadow of hesitation, that I would quite gladly be wrongfully accused of street soliciting, submit to medical examination, be mistakenly detained in prison or any other indignity, if by so doing I knew I lessened by ever so little the chance of a syphilitic child being born.

Is the evil to remain uncorrected from one generation to another? That is the question. Uncorrected evil multiplies itself, and the sum is a huge national disaster. I wish passionately that I had greater powers to make you see what to me is so plain. The mistake has been the muddle-headed thinking that sets apart these diseases from all other sicknesses of our bodies, obscuring the plain and comparatively simple question of cure with the entirely opposed problem of punishment; a confusion and losing of the way that leads inevitably into a forest-tangle of difficulty and unanswerable questions. And this heritage of wrong-thinking has compassed our feet, binding them and throwing us down, as soon as we try to move on, always hindering reform from generation to generation, and, until that entanglement is broken through, by bringing into it the light of honest thinking, the evil will go on, unchecked by our futile tearings here and there at withered branches. The supporting stem will continue to flourish and the devastating diseases will be spread.

(See Sir G. Archdall Reid's letter in Appendix.)

FOOTNOTES:

[117:1] See Ed. Carpenter, "Civilisation: Its Cause and Cure."

[129:1] The Conference was held in the ball-room of the Club of the Allied Officers at Cannes.

[129:2] In this connection, it should be noted that there was a time when syphilis was unknown in our civilisation. It cannot be traced with any certainty in Europe before the fifteenth century, although its origin is involved in some controversy. The attempt to suppress venereal diseases by proper treatment is of little more than twelve years duration. Three men—Wassermann, Ehrlich, and Noguchi—have supplied the knowledge whereby the evil may be attacked. See "Motherhood and the Relationship of the Sexes," p. 283, *et seq*.

[132:1] "The Fight against Venereal Disease," by Raymond B. Hodick, *The New Republic*, Nov. 30, 1918.

[134:1] My own opinions have been greatly influenced by what has been done in England with regard to drink, and in the American Army in maintaining the health of the Army by restricting prostitution, which explains a change in my attitude, since writing the chapter on "Prostitution" in *The Truth about Woman*.

[141:1] On this question the testimony of the American Army is urgent. They say, "Prophylaxis is under favorable circumstances secondary only in effectiveness to actual prevention of exposure.... When every other means have been used to make contact difficult if not impossible, prophylaxis, while not one hundred per cent. efficient, is invaluable as a last resort, and has contributed a large share towards maintaining in our Army the lowest venereal disease rate ever before known." Article before cited.

FIFTH ESSAY

IF A CHILD COULD CHOOSE?

A PLEA FOR PROTECTION FOR THE ILLEGITIMATELY BORN CHILD.

"I have called and ye refused; I have stretched out my hand and no man regarded."—Pro. i. 24.

I

Circumstances, at different times, have made me think and care very deeply about the injustice suffered by children born outside the protection of legal marriage; it was, indeed, when I was still young—young in experience and very ignorant of life; long before I began to write, at the time when I was headmistress of a private school for girls, that the question first forced itself into my consciousness.

It was in this way. I was told suddenly that the parents of two sisters who had entered my school as boarders were living together without being married. I was requested to send the children away. I can recall the scene through the length of the years; the excitement of the parent who was my informer; the kind of curious enjoyment she displayed in telling me the story, an enjoyment which surprised me so much and angered me at the time, but which, of course, is so easy to account for. I did not understand then those "ever-moving and so to speak immortal wishes of our Unconscious,"[151:1] residing in us all, ready to break loose and force some expression in our daily lives.

I am glad to know that young and ignorant as I was my quick instinctive dislike to this moral mud-raking helped and saved me. I would not send the two children away, and refused to take any notice whatever of their illegal birth.

I can hear still the sharp, surprised notes of Mrs. X's unpleasant voice as she turned to me and asked: "Now, Miss Gasquoine Hartley, what are you going to do?" How great was her amazement when I answered "Nothing!" She urged the necessity for action on account of my position and for the welfare of the school; pleaded the possible hurt done to her own children and all the other pupils. "You must be sensible," she insisted, "and send these bastards away. Of course, it is very sad for them, and one would not like to have to do it, but the sins of the parents," etc., etc.... You know the kind of beastly hypocritical talk. I need not continue.

Although I had no vivid realization at that time of the injustice of this view, anger sprang up hot within me. I was rude. I told Mrs. X that she might take her daughters away from my school; that I was willing for her to tell her beastly story to the parents of all my other pupils; that then they, if they wished to do so, might remove their daughters, as for me, I would continue my school with two pupils—the children she had told me were bastards.

I rather fancy, so ignorant was I then, that this was the first time I had heard that word "bastard," at any rate I felt the word emotionally, in a sharp and different way, when I heard it applied to little children, whom I knew and loved, was caring for and teaching. In this way, the greatest good was done me. I was made to feel. And when, in the later years of my life, I was brought by circumstances to consider the fate of the illegitimately born child, I was prepared already to understand the unprotected helplessness of these unfortunate little ones. I fully realized the cruel uncertainty that dogs like a foul shadow their young footsteps, the shame of their unhonored birth, which separates them from other children (and a child suffers so terribly from being separated, dislikes so passionately being different from its companions), shame that may always be brought suddenly as a hindrance against them, so that, even under the most favorable circumstances, they live in danger; grow up sensitive and passionately possessive, because so many things all other children have by right, relations who really are relations, a father and the right to use his name, a birth-certificate that does not record their parents' sin, are demanded from them in vain, so that at every turn they must fear the sword of contempt, against which they have no shield.

II

In many ways the position of the illegitimately born child, always sufficiently bad, has been rendered worse under war conditions. For one thing, their number has increased; the illegitimate birth-rate has steadily gone up in the war years and now is the highest on record.[153:1] And although it is easily possible to exaggerate the action of sexual irregularities, manifestly there can be no doubt that this war has acted directly as, indeed, war always does in increasing illegitimate births. Indirectly also the effect, after a war of such magnitude as this one has been, must be even greater in the immediate future in consequence of the resultant inequality of the sexes. All other factors determinant of illegitimacy are really dependent on the ratio of the number of unmarried males capable of paternity to the number of unmarried women capable of maternity in the community at a given time. Whenever the circle of nubile women surrounding the virile male becomes larger, there will be a corresponding increase in the number of illegitimately born children.[154:1]

A further difficulty, very pressing at the present time, arises from the fact that the supply of reliable foster-mothers has diminished everywhere, especially in London and the large cities. Even where women suitable for this purpose are still attainable, the weekly sum asked for the child's keep is so high that in spite of increased wages and the raising from 5/- to 10/- of the maximum amount allowed against the father under an affiliation order, few mothers can afford to pay it and live decently themselves. The bitter cry of the driven mother frequently is, "Help me to get rid of my baby."

We have demanded too much from the unmarried mother. As a rule she is very young. She is faced with an almost

C. Gasquoine Hartley

impossible task, and often she is weak in character, incapable, without guidance of so difficult a duty as the up-bringing of the little creature she has helped so greatly to wrong by its very birth.

III

For let no one make a mistake. There is a sin of illegitimacy, which, indeed, I would emphasize as strongly as I am able. Irresponsible parenthood must always be immoral, and the mother's sin is greater than is that of the father. I must insist upon this, though I realize how unpopular such a view will be to many women. But the mother, through her closer connection with the child, must bear the deeper responsibility for its birth, a responsibility that can be traced back and back to the very lowest forms of life. The insect mother does not fail to place her offspring—the children she will never see—in a position chosen most carefully to ensure their future protection, and to achieve this good frequently she sacrifices her life. Shall the human mother, then, be held guiltless when she shows no forethought for the future of her child?

C. Gasquoine Hartley

IV

The English law has always looked with great disfavor on the illegitimately born child. A bastard is *filius nullius*, "nobody's child." He cannot be legitimized even on the subsequent marriage of his parents. In Scotland this injustice is not found. There (as also in every other civilized land except our own) the child becomes legitimized by the simple natural process of the father marrying the mother. Can the cruelty of our English law have any positive value? It is difficult to think so. At common law the illegitimate can have no guardian, he has no relations and no rights of inheritance; he is given unprotected into the custody of his mother, and until the age of fourteen is wholly in her power.

Here we have a clear duty, and another case of the urgent need of a readjustment of our moral attitude, of a change in our laws and in our judgments strictly parallel to several we have considered. Once more I am convinced of the poverty, and selfishness, and the immorality of our views. Nor do I find great improvement to-day over yesterday. There is much talk and some tinkering, but though our judgments are less harsh, still we are choked with the weeds of false sentiment and feminine egoism. We fail to attack straight and think boldly.

The sin of illegal parenthood is really a collective concern: to turn our backs on the pitiable plight of these children, to refuse to fulfill our duties toward them, is to leave them entirely to those who are often least fitted to help them, and also to open up direct ways to every kind of wickedness. And it follows, almost necessarily, if we accept this view of our collective responsibility, that the greatest danger in the present position arises out of our selfish plan of leaving these children unprotected in the hands of their mothers, giving them no other legal relations, making no fixed provision for their guardianship, allowing each mother to do as she likes; to establish paternity or leave the child unfathered, to keep the child with her or give it into the care of strangers, to make any kind of arrangements, good, bad, or none at all, for its education and upbringing. And what makes it the more intolerable is the indifference of almost all of us to what is done, or is not done, by the mother. The subject is difficult and unpleasant: illegitimacy is wicked and, therefore, must not be talked about. If any case comes to our notice, we hush it up. We are too selfish and lazy to attack the deep causes of the evil—to remove temptation; instead, we directly encourage evil; we place the illegitimately born child in a position of such disadvantage that its future existence is jeopardized.

C. Gasquoine Hartley

V

You will probably say that I am focusing all attention on the illegitimate mother, and am not considering the responsibility of the illegitimate father. I grant this, and I am doing it with fixed intention. I want to consider the problem of illegitimacy from this definite,[158:1] and as I am aware, restricted point of view, carefully and very thoroughly to look at it from this one side only, in order to show others, if I can, what I have found to be true: the urgent need there is to take the illegitimately born child from its mother's authority. I would refer my readers to my other books and writings, where again and again I set forth, as urgently as I know how, the drastic changes I would advocate in our bastardy and affiliation laws, in order to bind the illegitimate father to his duty and thus prevent profligacy being as easy as to-day it is. I do not want to go over this ground again. But mark this: the stigma attaching to the fatherhood of all illegitimate children is, at present, the strongest direct cause of neglect of his duties by the man; his failure to stand by the mother and pay for the support of the child. He may be willing to do his duty in both these ways, but not if it involves the abandonment of his entire career. With public opinion so determined, immoral, irresponsible conduct is almost inevitable. But this opens up, of course, a whole series of different questions, which, for the reasons I have just set forth, I do not try to answer, rather purposely neglecting the second illegitimate parent, the father, so as better to focus attention on the evils arising from the existing unprotected relations between the mother and the child.

And I would urge further, with all the power that I have, the need for considering this aspect of the problem, for it is one that is very much neglected. I know it is very unpopular with the majority of those who care most earnestly about the unmarried mother.

It is to be wished that this question also could be approached free from all falseness of modern feminist sentimentality. The great hindrance to straight thinking is the same here as in so many other of the moral problems we have been considering: that desire for personal possessions, which so often is a treachery against the universal good. I care for nothing really except the saving of the child, and I cannot regard the child as the possession of the mother. So many women seem to take for themselves the right to claim power over a child by virtue of the suffering through which they passed to bring it into the world; although surely this should be denied when conception takes place carelessly and without any kind of forethought for the birth that may follow. I will not, however, wait to say more, my position will, I hope, become plainer as I proceed. *It is an assertion of the child's right to special protection and care in order that it may be saved from the cruel injustice of having to pay the penalty of its mother's carelessness and lack of maternal responsibility.*[161:1]

C. Gasquoine Hartley

VI

Since the law of 1834 a woman has been legally liable to maintain her natural child until it reaches the age of sixteen. She is allowed to establish paternity, and, if she can do this, to obtain a maintenance order against the father, the maximum amount now allowed being 10/- a week, which sum is to be paid until the child reaches the age of sixteen. But the mother is not compelled to take this course, indeed, she is hindered from doing so in every possible way, both by the many absurd difficulties of the law and the expense of the summons. And this is the cause of clear injustice to the child, whose right to a father and to support from him ought not to be dependent on the caprice of the mother, whose desire is often to protect the man rather than to do justice to the child. For this reason the establishment of paternity should be compulsory on the mother or her relations as it now is in Norway. Every child has a right to a father as well as to a mother.

The ante-natal conditions of these babies are obviously of the very worst. All those months when a woman most requires special rest, special quiet, and, in particular, special mental repose, will be spent in anxiety and fear. In too many cases the girl has to keep herself, and it is mighty difficult to get a job without a character. And, here, let me point out to those who believe vaguely that a "love-child" is a finer type than other children, that this is true only in so far as the atmosphere in which the mother spends her pregnancy is one of love and undisturbed calm. Do let us face the facts of the situation.

Often the baby is born wherever the driven mother can find shelter, the baby's interests in the matter being certainly of no account then or later. In the eyes of the law the child is without rights and belongs to no one. In the eyes of our Christian society he is a "branded outcast," in the eyes of his mother too often he is but a mark of her shame: conditions of injustice to the child that must too often result in the growing up of a poor type of child.

It has been found that illegitimates at birth are quite as hardy as legitimate children; they would even seem to be born stronger, since they die, unlike the legitimate, more frequently in the *second* month than the *first*; and more frequently in the *third* than in the *second* month. The deferred and insufficient regulation of the child's diet, the frequent failure on the part of the father to provide the means of support, the not uncommon indifference on the part of the mother towards her child's welfare, and the necessity of placing the child in cheap care, are the chief causes of the high mortality rates among illegitimate children.

Even in the few fortunate cases where the maximum alimony is claimed and granted to the mother, there is no certainty that the weekly payments will be continued and regularly paid throughout the child's growing years, and though there is improvement in this direction since the Affiliation Orders Act, 1914, and the appointment of a Collecting Officer, there is still far too easy opportunity for the escape of a shirking father. The law takes no cognizance of the fact that in the majority of cases it is an absolute impossibility for the mothers, even with the best will in the world, unassisted, to place their children in proper conditions for their up-bringing. At present, with no authorized person to supervise the mother and check her absolute control, to see how she spends the alimony, where she places the child, what education it has, what prospects of growing into an effective adult; too often the child never reaches maturity and its case is often worse if it does survive; its home changed from one place to another, sometimes with the mother, sometimes

C. Gasquoine Hartley

boarded out with irresponsible people, or adopted with a premium, it is liable to gross neglect and the most far-reaching and incurable perversions of character.

We have reached this truth then. _The urgent duty that rests with the law and with us all is the duty of taking action to prevent as far as it is possible, and in every way that we can, the penalty of its illegitimate birth being paid by the child._

VII

Now, this is not going to be done as easily as it may seem; and before it can be done, in my opinion, we shall have to clear our minds from a serious error, to which we cling with feminist tentacles in order to indulge the sentiment so passionately clung to by women-reformers of the mother's right to her child.

You will have noted how strongly I have insisted on illegitimacy being the sin of the parents—of the mother even more than of the father—and have refused to use the word in connection with the child. I have done this, as must already be plain, for a clear reason. I wished to mark the separation of the child from its parents' sin. I did not do it from a perverse refusal to accept what is usually accepted. Clearly it is absurd to brand the child "illegitimate," since it can never be the fault of any child that its parents brought it into the world. Let us talk, if you like, of illegitimate mothers, also of illegitimate fathers, but never again of the illegitimate child. The penalty of the parents' sin must not be paid by the child. I cannot emphasize this too often or too strongly.

The child must be saved by special protection.

Now, it seems to be taken for granted by all modern reformers that the best way to do this and to serve the interests of the child is to make even closer than it is at present the connection of the mother and the child, keeping them more certainly together, except in the few cases when such a course is clearly absolutely impossible, and *under all circumstances* regarding the separation of any mother from her baby as "an exceptional and deplorable necessity."[166:1]

C. Gasquoine Hartley

What I have said already will make it abundantly evident that I cannot accept this view. I feel convinced that it is founded on a feeling of sentiment for the mother rather than on a desire for justice to the child. This tendency to confuse two separate issues has been marked in all the numerous recent discussions of the unmarried mother. I have heard the strongest indignation expressed by feminist speakers whose sentiment bubbles from them like a pan of porridge boiling over. "The child should be brought up in the atmosphere of the mother's love"; "Mother and child should not be separated," this is the opinion repeated again and again, and *always without qualification as to the character of the mother.* Even those few workers who realize the situation much more as it presents itself to me, from the standpoint of the child's welfare, and therefore advocate the placing of all illegitimately born children under "authorized protective oversight," yet cling to the sentiment that it is "best for the child to remain with its mother." They apprehend the difficulty of the mother's character—or rather want of character—but they do not take the necessary bold step out of this net of sentiment, and face the truth that, in many cases, the first and great enemy from whom those ill-used little ones have to be protected is their mother.

Unmarried mothers are overwhelmingly preponderant among the frivolous and weak-willed. This will be an unpopular statement to feminist sentiment; few women are honest in facing this question, though probably they do not know that they are dishonest. We women need to be more careful in accepting the over-hasty view that these illegitimate mothers in any large numbers are good girls who have been led astray by men. This view, once held by me in common with most women, I have been compelled to give up. Seduction cannot, I am sure, be accepted without very great caution as a common cause for illegitimate births. My experience has taught me that nervous instability, the result often of monotonous or too exhausting work, leading quickly to a desire for excitement and effort to escape dullness, as also love of finery and joy in receiving presents, are the principal motives that lead girls into illegal relations. And what I want to make plain is this: a characterless girl, irresponsible, without care for the future, drifting, snatching at pleasure, taking the easiest course—this is the girl who bears a child illegitimately and this is the girl incapable of becoming a good mother.

This characterless irresponsibility of the average unmarried mother is known to every social worker. The difficulty is dwelt upon in the reports of rescue homes and police-workers. I have read many separate articles which refer to it. "Temperamental instability," as it is fittingly called, inevitably makes capable motherhood impossible. True, these unmarried mothers may, and frequently do, "pour out a wealth of pent-up affection on the child," but often she will do this for half-an-hour and neglect it for days afterwards. Those who talk here of the "mother's right to her child" are being misled by sentiment. Women of the prostitute type, whose love and tears are on the surface, must not be judged too tenderly as capable of great improvement. The child may "steady the mother for a time,"[169:1] but the mother will probably by her carelessness, bad example, helplessness and inefficiency unsteady the child for life.

And it is this that matters. Yes, matters to you, my readers, and to me and to us all. The child illegitimately born is to become a future citizen; and it is not good for society to permit its mother to endanger its future. We—the other members of Society—must object to such a possibility, we cannot allow it to be tolerated on any grounds of sentiment. We object from humane care for the child, but also from patriotism and enlightened self-interest; for the consequences of the mother's unguided mistakes in training must fall on

C. Gasquoine Hartley

someone, and in this country they fall chiefly on the rate-payers.

I shall not wait to give you the many and overwhelming facts and figures that I could bring forward in support of these statements. To-day all the pitiful statistics of illegitimate births are widely known; at least they are known intellectually, though I doubt their being known emotionally, which is quite another matter and whips our indifference into action. Only the workers in the darkest places of our great cities know how large illegitimacy looms as a factor in the social disintegration that leads to the prison, to the mad-house, to the hospitals, to the casual wards, and to the streets. Only the eye of the scientist can vision in the relation of the unhonored child to its mother the seed of that evil which one day shall become the dishonor of the dishonorable man.[170:1]

VIII

I can foresee an objection that will be made: it will be urged that much of what I say of the unfitness of the average unmarried mother to train her child is equally applicable to the average married mother. True: I agree. There is, however, this all important difference. The child of the married woman is not placed, either by circumstances or by the law, in the power of its mother. It has a second parent: even if the father is dead and its mother is the only parent, the home is watched by grandmother, by grandfather—perhaps by four grandparents, by sharp-eyed aunts and encouraging uncles; probably there are brothers and sisters, cousins, great-aunts and great-cousins. There will also be a more or less extensive circle of criticizing friends. Thus the baby is surrounded from its birth by watchers—a veritable host of unpaid inspectors. Now, you see my point and understand the immense difference. It is the terrible loneliness of the child born illegitimately, outside the safe publicity of marriage, without relations, belonging by right to nobody, that makes the power given by law to its mother so dangerous.

That is why I would plead, with every power that I have, that we leave sentiment behind us as we approach this question. We are a hopelessly sentimental nation, and we cling to platitudes as a half naked beggar will cling to his tattered shirt. We collect moral antiquities. Inherited and worn-out ideas, psychological fossils, moral survivals, these must be treasured only in romance; they must be deleted from life. Every moral rule, every sentiment, as also every institution, must be tested, from period to period, to see if it works still in a practical and healthful direction to help the individual to do right and for the betterment of the race.

C. Gasquoine Hartley

IX

We English are sentimental.

Perhaps it is worth while to wait a moment to ask the cause of this deeply-acting English sentimentality. It rests on two qualities, our moderation and our exclusiveness. But the precise causes of these qualities are not so certain; the English are romantic, but our moderation prevents us being too impulsively romantic; on the other hand, our homely *feeling for reality* does not lead us to investigate reality too deeply. We dislike the sordid and the "not nice." We are imaginative and passionate, but our imaginations and passions are carefully balanced by reasons and calm reflections. We are kindly, but not to the extent of saintlike self-sacrifice; also we are selfish, but again not to the extent of brutal egoism. Our exclusiveness makes "Birds of a feather flock together" and at the same time fosters our ignorance of, and indifference to, the existence of any other species of bird. Thus the good know nothing of the bad; the people who drink, play bridge, dance and have a fashionably good time, for instance, have hardly heard of the meeting-frequenting, soul-worrying reformers who live in Garden Suburbs. Thus in England there is very little to disturb a comfortable feeling; protected by our moderation and exclusiveness, there is no force inside from ourselves, or outside from observers, to make us revise our position, consider the right or the wrong of our moral attitude, to give up our illusions of comfort. That is one reason why we so often stand aside from the ugly reality of things as they are, "hold high the banner of the ideal," which is the untruthful way in which we allude to things as we want them to be.

X

Now, all this leads up very directly to the special aspect of the problem we are considering. We have to realize just what are the results likely to follow from the close relationship of mother and child in the case of the illegitimately born. Personally, I am certain that in most cases the situation is one of quite appalling dangers.

I cannot feel sure that even the most helpful supervision of the mother, if she and her child enter a hostel, or other institution, can, in the majority of cases, save some hurt, if her character is unsteady, being given by her to the child. We are only just now coming at all to understand how immensely fateful to the whole later development are the first few years of infant life, and further, how everything is colored—it would be truer to say "decided"—by the character and actions of the mother; how any hurt done, or mistake made then, can never be undone. Even an unwise expression of too fond and emotional affection may act to cause ruin in the after years. All who have even a slight acquaintance with the enlightening work of Freud, will know the folly of "trying to save the illegitimate mother through the agency of the child."

Let me state the case quite plainly: *There are different types among these unmarried mothers, just as there are among married mothers, some would be wise mothers did we give them the necessary help and opportunity, but many would not be wise mothers under any circumstances or with any amount of help, because they are weak in character and are incapable of child-training. Now, the problem of saving the child is quite a different one in these opposite cases: in the one instance everything ought to be done to keep the child with its mother, in the other the one safeguard is to keep the*

C. Gasquoine Hartley

child wholly out of the mother's power.

I state sadly, but without hesitation, and from my own experience, that in innumerable cases the salvation of the child depends more than anything else on its complete separation from the mother. I cannot countenance sentiment that blinds our intelligence. How can it be wise to recommend in cases where the character of the mother "seems to warrant a separation," that "periodic visiting by the mother needs to be fostered."[175:1] Again, what must happen if the baby is in the care of the trained nurse by day, but at night is given up to the untrained and often untrainable mother, who goes out to work but returns to the hostel to sleep?[175:2]

You will tell me the mother wants to have the child. That is right and good from one point of view—that of the mother; but from the other—the point of view of the child—it cannot work out well. The child switches hither and thither between various treatments and quite opposite influences. And with the child's terrible candor it shows the hurt it is suffering and says always, in effect, though not in words, "I wish you would all agree as to how you want me to grow up."

I may state the question in this way: *Do we want the child to grow up like its mother or do we want to save it from being like her?*

To answer this simple question will help us more than at first we may see. Frankly, our confusion here in fixing what we want is the cause which, in my opinion, more than anything else must bring failure to what is being done, and being proposed to be done, to help the illegitimately born child. Our sentiment causes us to confuse what is good for the mother with what is good for the child, and, because of this, we are failing to grapple with the most warring element in the whole difficult problem of saving the child; we shall have to face and deal successfully with this certain fact of the very common unfitness of the unmarried mother, before we can do the one simple and right thing and prevent the child from having to pay the penalty of its parents' illegitimate act. We are brought back always to this: the saving of the child as the one plain duty before us.

C. Gasquoine Hartley

XI

In a previous section I dealt with the harmful way in which circumstances and the law, acting together, place the child born out of wedlock wholly and terribly in the mother's power. But there is a further aspect of the situation now to be considered. I wish to show how destructively that power may act, stimulated in some cases by an unwise affection as well as in others where no mother-love seems present, and act for years to hurt and even destroy the child. To establish this and make the facts plainer, I will now tell in detail a few cases of illegitimate motherhood from my own knowledge. You will see then exactly what I mean and how dangerous to the child is the power held by these unwatched mothers; the facts of the case will, I hope, speak to you more emotionally, and therefore more forcibly, than any further statement of my own opinion.

Case 1.—A baby girl was born to a young mother of unstable though not altogether bad character. The father was a gentleman: he did not seduce the girl. He paid the expenses of the confinement and afterwards, and with the mother's consent, placed the little one with good country people, paying for her support. For more than a year and a half the baby lived with its foster mother and grew up a very healthy and joyous little girl. The real mother visited the child and showed most emotional love for her. One day, without reason and without warning, she took the child away. The foster-mother appealed to the father; he did all in his power to have the child returned, and finally, when the mother refused, said he would make no further contribution for the support of the child. He knew the mother was unfit to bring up the child, but he could do nothing to prevent her action. The mother took the child to another town. What she did with the little one is not fully known, but when, after nine months, the foster-mother traced her, she was in a most pitiable condition of dirt and neglect, and, what was much worse, she was terribly frightened. Quite plainly she had been beaten and ill-used. The mother was not poor, so that cannot be made an excuse.

The foster-mother offered now to adopt the child and bring it up as her own. Her offer was accepted by the mother, but with the provision, which unfortunately was granted, that she should still come to see the child. Her visits always affected the child unfavorably.

During the next three years the little girl found renewed health and peace in her happy adopted home. Then her enemy—her mother—again took her away. For a year she kept this delicate, nervous and well-brought-up child with her in London under very adverse circumstances. Then she went off, leaving her daughter, now five years old, with no proper person to care for her and quite without means of support.

Case 2.—A girl of loose character, but not a regular prostitute, found herself pregnant. She did not know certainly who among her lovers was the father, but she decided on one man, who she knew was not the father. He was rich and kind, or rather as she told me "he was a softy." Accordingly she told him the baby was his. He arranged for the confinement, afterwards he took the baby and the mother to live in the home of his mother. They were kindly treated in every way, and the baby flourished. But the mother was bored by goodness: one day she went off: she did not take the baby. Unfortunately she left a letter—not I fear from conscience, but from mischief and a desire to insult goodness—telling the man she had tricked him and he was not the father of the child. The man was angry, disliking the knowledge of his having been duped; his mother was still

C. Gasquoine Hartley

more angry. Once more the child was the sufferer. It was sent away from the happy and rich home to an institution.

Case 3.—A working-class girl, belonging to a respectable country family, gave birth to a baby girl. The father was a soldier, but the girl did not know his name or where he was. During her confinement and afterward she remained at home with her mother and brother. The baby was ailing and became ill. The brother told his sister, the mother, that she must take it to the Infirmary in the neighboring town. She objected on the ground that she would have to go in with the baby. However, the brother insisted and arranged to meet her and the baby at the Infirmary gates the following evening. His sister was there, but not the baby. She told him that a friend was going to take care of the baby for her. The baby was never heard of again.

Case 4.—This time the mother was highly born and educated, but she belonged naturally to the promiscuous type of lover: she ought to have been a prostitute. She had many lovers and was strongly sexual, not passionate so much as voluptuous. By one of her lovers, and by mistake, a child was conceived, and though attempts were made to get rid of the mistake, a boy was born, fairly healthy. The father, a modern tired profligate, refused to accept the responsibilities of his fatherhood, though he did not deny the child was his, and continued as one of the lovers of its mother. The mother showed no sign of maternal love; the little one was much neglected and probably would have died, but, when about two months old, he was taken from the mother and cared for and most tenderly loved by one of the woman's other lovers. He left her as her indifference to her child killed his affection, but he took her child to bring up as his own son.

Case5.—A record of this very revolting case appeared recently in the daily papers under the heading "L8000

Baby's End." I copy the story as it was told in the "Daily Mail": the date I do not remember.

"The love affair of a middle-aged painter, Charles Godin, with his model Georgette Belli, aged 16, has led to a remarkable charge of murder. Georgette became a mother, and when the painter died a few months later he left the child L8000.

"The girl married a young man named Emile Gourdon, and the baby was placed in the care of a grandmother. Later, when the young mother wished to get back her child, the grandmother refused to give it up on the ground that the young couple meant to destroy it in order to inherit the money, and produced letters and telegrams in support of her suspicion. Georgette, however, got an order from a court for the surrender of the baby, and went to live at Marseilles with her husband.

"One day, while walking on the jetty, the woman appeared to stumble and the child fell into the sea and was drowned. The couple have been arrested, the woman, it is alleged, having pretended to faint in order to make away with her child."

Now, I know that these five cases I have recounted are not exceptional, though some of their sordid details may be specially disagreeable. Give but a moment's attention to the facts that stand out, and at once you will grasp what is wrong. We are demanding too much from these unmarried mothers, and, by leaving the full power of parenthood in their weak hands, are jeopardizing the child's safety; we are also encouraging conditions harmful to society. It is like leaving a loaded gun in the hands of a little child. These cases speak for themselves. In No. 3 and No. 5 the child was killed by the direct act of the mother; in the former case there was some excuse from the harsh rule that the sick baby of an unmarried mother cannot be received into a hospital unless the mother goes in with it (the reason of this, of course, being that the mother will use this means of ridding herself of the baby) and will never come to reclaim it; but in the horrible case of No. 5 there is no ray of excuse. This case is especially interesting because it makes so abundantly plain the terrible need there is for the immediate establishment of safe legal adoption. In cases No. 2 and No. 4 we have the curious situation, by no means so uncommon as many might think, of the wrong man acting the part of father to an illegitimately born child; in the one case this was done through the trickery of the mother and was but temporary, the child suffering, while in the other case, more interesting and less common, vicarious fatherhood was voluntarily adopted. I would ask you to note that in none of the five cases was bad motherhood caused by poverty and home-lessness. So frequently it is said: "Give these mothers a chance, and their mother-love will blossom like the rose"— or some similar and unproved tosh. It is not true. The good mother may be a bad mother by adverse circumstances, this I acknowledge readily, but that the most favorable circum-stances can make the bad mother into a good mother, I emphatically deny. This is why it is so unsafe and so wrong of society to leave the child unprotected and unwatched, for the mother to do with it what she likes.

The first case, because it shows so clearly the adverse action of the mother's influence is, in my opinion, most instructive among the five cases I have given. Such changeableness on the mother's part, and interference with the child is just what is likely, and most often does take place, and will go on taking place, until the law protects these children by effective guardianship. I would specially point out that this mother was not in the least indifferent to her baby. If you had talked to her, probably your sentiment would have burned and glowed about the hardness of her case in being separated from her baby, and you would have said wonderful platitudes about the beauty of a mother's love. And yet the shameful hurt she did to her child can never be undone. Her undisciplined love was the cause of the child's undoing.

I have now, I hope, made it sufficiently plain why the illegitimately born child should no longer be considered as belonging to the mother, but should be recognized as a member of society, and, as such, entitled to protection, so that it may suffer as little, and not as much, as is possible from the disadvantages of its illegal birth. This is plain justice. Yet before it can be done we shall need an immediate and great reform of our bad and antiquated bastardy and affiliation laws. We shall need also a change of heart.

XII

I shall be asked what changes I would suggest. The answer is not easy: it is not so much a question of altering this regulation or that, of removing hindrances and giving increased help; that is good, but more is needed: we want a change of the entire system: *the firm understanding that the clear aim before us is to place the child, as nearly as this can be done, in the same position of advantage as it would have had if it had not been illegally born. If there must be punishments, let them fall on the parents, never on the child.*

Now, how can this best be done? In the space I can devote here, it is possible only to throw out a few suggestions.

First, and I think exceedingly important, the law should take account of the attitude of the father. In all cases where the paternity of the child is acknowledged openly by the man and with the mother, and guarantees are given that the duties of both parents will be faithfully fulfilled, the child should be legitimized, receive the name of the father, be qualified to inherit from him, and in every way given the same rights as the legitimate child, even if the parents are unable or do not wish to marry. This opportunity of right conduct once given to men by the law, I believe that many, who are fathers illegitimately, would voluntarily take this course and gladly acknowledge and fulfill the responsibilities of their fatherhood.

In all other cases, in which paternity is not voluntarily acknowledged, I take the most important duty of the law to be the official appointment of guardians. I believe nothing else is so urgently needed to protect these fatherless little ones. Such guardianship[187:1] could be provided without great difficulty or expense if *each illegitimately born child,*

*not openly acknowledged and willingly provided for by its
father, was made a ward of the Court of Summary
Jurisdiction in the district in which it lived and thus placed
under authoritative supervision. The child would, by the
authority of the Court, be boarded out (1) with the mother in
all cases where her health, character and previous records
were such as to make this arrangement the best for the child,
(2) in hostels, either with the mother or without her, (3) with
paid foster-parents, (4) with adopted parents. In every case
regular visitation of the child would be necessary, and the
child must not be removed from one home to another or any
change made with regard to it without the authority of the
Court, which shall have power (1) to appoint guardians,
either in addition to, or substitution for the mother of the
child; (2) to approve any scheme for the education or
training of the child, and at all times and in all ways to
exercise authority in every matter pertaining to the child's
welfare.*[188:1]

I would wish for a further restriction, which, however hardly
it may seem to bear on the mother, is, in my opinion, most
necessary for safeguarding the child. It is this: *If the child by
the decision of the Court is boarded out with foster parents,
permanently adopted or placed in a home apart from the
mother, no interference or even visiting by the mother shall
be permitted except at the discretion of the Court.*

I would suggest that in every town or rural district guardians
should be appointed (preferably a man and a woman) either
paid or voluntary, but officially appointed: all that is needed
is an extension of the duties of the Collecting Officer,
appointed under the Affiliation Orders Act of 1914. This
officer already takes out of the mother's hands the work of
collecting the weekly payments granted under a maintenance
order, and he also has certain powers of enforcing payments
from a defaulting father. But at present his taking action is

dependent on the desire of the mother. His duties ought in all cases to be compulsory. They would be (1) to help the mother before and after the birth of the child; (2) to seek out the father and urge a voluntary acknowledgment of his paternity, and, when this cannot be gained, to see that the law is rightly administered so that full alimony may be obtained; (3) to watch over the interests of the child and see that the decisions of the Court are carried out without interference from the mother.

The kind of help given would have to be varied and must be made suitable to each individual case, but every child would be a ward of the guardians in the district in which it lived, and would be regularly visited. I would suggest further that there should be placed over these visiting-guardians a Government-appointed, permanent, highly salaried official— a kind of over-guardian-parent or Consultant, who would supervise the work of the ordinary guardians in difficult cases, and advise as to the best means of administering the law. This high official ought, in my opinion, to be a woman.

Such a scheme as I have outlined (briefly and, I know, inadequately) would achieve the three-fold purpose of (1) safeguarding the child, (2) guiding and helping the mother, (3) fastening responsibility on the father. If wisely administered by guardians, acting with sympathy and understanding, it could hardly fail to achieve the desired result of protecting the child. Every illegitimately born child would be placed in a position of safety.

As a preliminary step, and pending legislation, it would be an excellent plan if groups of interested people, or societies, were to form local representative committees to appoint voluntary Visiting-guardians. By this means the plan could be tried, and some kind of responsible and authoritative guardianship at once undertaken. We ought to do this now, for death and suffering to the little children are going on while we delay.

There is no more for me to say.

The saving of these little ones is a plain duty upon me and upon you, my readers. Let us clear hardness from our minds and sentiment from our hearts; both will equally lead us astray. The child is the real care of the State and of us all; it is the child who is dependent; the child who has been sinned against; the child we have to protect. Save these babies from death and from life that is worse than death; give these children a right start in life. Let no illegitimately born child be able to say in after years, "I have called and ye refused; I have stretched out my hand and no man regarded."

FOOTNOTES:

[151:1] Freud.

[153:1] The illegitimate percentage of total births for the first half of 1918 was 6 per cent., in 1914 it was 4.24 per cent.

[154:1] See article by Havelock Ellis. *The New Statesman*, May 25th, 1918. Also Prinzing, whom Ellis quotes.

[158:1] In an article which appeared in *Maternity and Child Welfare*, in 1918, I first brought this question forward: the article was in answer to a discussion which had previously taken place in that useful and excellent little journal on the Unmarried Mother and her Child. I shall use some portion of what I then said in this essay, because I think my arguments would be weakened if I tried to re-write them.

[161:1] I do not include the father here, because under the English law the mother is the only parent.

[166:1] See Pamphlet issued by the *National Council for the Unmarried Mother and her Child*, page 8.

[169:1] These and similar statements are brought forward as reason for keeping mother and child together. I need scarcely say they leave me unmoved.

[170:1] See an excellent article on "The Love Child In Germany and Austria," *English Review*, June, 1912.

[175:1] Article on "The Illegitimate Child," *Maternity and Child Welfare*, September, 1917. One of the articles I was asked to answer.

[175:2] This is the plan advocated by the National Council for Unmarried Mothers.

[187:1] Some years ago the city of Leipsic started an admirable scheme by which illegitimately born children automatically became the wards of officially appointed guardians.

[188:1] An excellent scheme has been drawn up and issued as a pamphlet by "The National Society for the Prevention of Cruelty to Children"—Occasional Papers V. *Illegitimate Children*.

SIXTH ESSAY

FORESEEING EVIL[193:1]

BEING CONCERNED WITH PASSIONATE FRIENDSHIPS, AND HOW RESPONSIBLE CONDUCT MAY BE ESTABLISHED IN SEXUAL RELATIONSHIPS OUTSIDE OF MARRIAGE.

"A prudent man foreseeth the evil, and hideth himself, but the   simple pass on and are punished."—Pro. xxxvii. 12.

I

All over the world women are restless; perhaps, in no direction is this shown more alarmingly than in the attitude of many modern girls toward marriage and motherhood. There is dissatisfaction brewing in sexual matters as well as in every other department of life, and only the hypocrites cry "Peace" when there is no peace.

I have said so much about this restlessness of women that I do not want to labor the question, rather I wish to consider what to me seem the results as they are finding expression in the relations of women and men. It is, of course, a subject

C. Gasquoine Hartley

much too difficult to allow arbitrary judgments, all I can do is to jot down a few remarks, rough notes, as it were, on what I have seen and thought.

And first, I would ask the reader to remember those many sex-conventions that in the past have gathered around women's lives. I need not enumerate them, they are known to you all, but what I want to emphasize is that, though so many of them have been removed their influence persists. Always the customs and beliefs of a past social life live on beneath the surface of society; in a thousand ways we do not recognize, they press upon the individual soul. We cannot without strong effort escape from the chains of our inheritance. In the nations of the West, where the bridegroom's joy with his bride is never spoken of except as a subject fit for jests, where celibacy has been extolled and marriage treated as "a remedy for sin," where barrenness instead of being regarded as the greatest possible evil is artificially produced, where the natural joys of the body—the sex-joys and the joy of wine and food have been confused with disgraceful things—it is there that a perpetual conflict lurks at the very heart of life; hidden it becomes more active for evil.

Always times of upheaval and change afford opportunities for escape in violent expression, and while we bewail the disorder and confusion, the many sexual crimes that are overwhelming us, we ought to take warning at our folly in having set up for ourselves the new fashionable god of "escape from sex."

Women are the worst sinners. At every opportunity the women of my generation have been insisting on "the monstrous exaggerations of the claims of sex," breaking away violently from the older obsessing preoccupation with their position as women, but only to take up new evasions—

fresh miserable attempts at escape. What began as a war of ideals became before long a chaos. It has had the effect not at all of minimizing the power of sex, but just as far as the deeper needs and instincts have been denied, has there been a deliberate turning on the part of the young to the reliefs of sex-excitements. The servitude of sex is one of the essential riddles of life. Personally I do not feel there is any simple solution. The conflict, broadly speaking, lies in this: our sex needs have changed very little through the ages, now we are faced with the task of adapting them to the society in which we find ourselves placed, of conforming with the rules laid down, accepting all the pressing claims of civilized life, conditions, not clearly thought out and established to help us and make moral conduct easier, but dependent much more on property, social rank, and ignorance,—all combining to make any kind of healthy sex expression more difficult, which explains our duplicity and so often prevents the acceptance in practice of the code of conduct upheld by most of us as right. I think it is a particularly intolerable state of affairs. It is not pleasant to find oneself out as a moral hypocrite.

The primitive savage within us all always will make any kind of excuse to break out in its own primitive savage way. We are just too civilized to face this, and, I think, there can be little doubt that our conduct has been hindered by many of the modern intellectual suppressions. The convention that passions and emotions are absent, when in reality they are present, to-day has broken down as, indeed, it always must break down everywhere, leading in thousands of cases individual young women and men to disaster, making us all more furtive, more pitiful slaves of the force whose power we are not yet sufficiently brave to acknowledge.

Much of our civilization has revealed itself as a monstrous sham, more dangerously indecent because of its pretense at

C. Gasquoine Hartley

decency. It is something like those poisoned tropical forests, fever-infested, which were in the land of my birth, beautiful outwardly, with great vivid flowers, high palms, towering trees of fern, all garlanded with creepers and lovely wild growth,—glades of fair shadow inviting to rest, yet poisonous so that to sleep there was death.

II

We have yet to find our way in sexual things. The revealing knowledge that Freud and his followers have given to the world shows us something of our groping darkness; there is much we have to relearn, to accept many things in ourselves and others that we have denied. We must give up our cherished pretense of the sexual life being easy and innocent, we must open doors into the secret defenses we have set around ourselves. None of us know much, but at least we must begin to tell the truth about the little we do know.

Now, this self-honesty may sound a simple thing. It is not. Few of us even know how hard it will be. It will call for the greatest possible courage to tear away the new, as well as the old, bandages with which we have blinkered our eyes, walking in shadow so complete that some of us have lost the very power of sight, like the strange fishes that live in the gloom of the Kentucky caves. Honesty will demand a real conversion, a change in our attitude to ourselves and to one another. We shall have, indeed, to reassure ourselves of the sincerity of our intentions, to begin as the first necessary step to accept ourselves as we are and to give up what we desire to pretend we are, to learn to be truthful to ourselves about ourselves.

Better to know ourselves as sinners, than to be virtuous in falsehood. We must grow up emotionally; want things to seem what they are, not what we want them to be. Afterwards we can perhaps go on to help others.

C. Gasquoine Hartley

III

There is a further danger to which I must refer, for it is one that, in my opinion, is very active for disaster. I find a tendency among most grown-ups, especially among teachers and advanced parents, who ought to know better, to place too firm a reliance on moral teaching and sexual enlightenment as a means of saving our daughters and our sons from making the same mistakes in their lives that we ourselves have made. Like those drowning in deep waters where they cannot swim, we have clutched at any plank of hope. You see, so many of the old planks—religion, social barriers, chaperons, home restrictions, and so many more, on which our parents used to rely, have failed us, broken in our hands by the vigorous destroying of the young generation, and, therefore we have clutched with frantic fingers at this new fair-looking life raft, in pursuit of the one aim to protect our children. Myself, I have done this. It is with uttermost sadness I have to acknowledge now that I do not believe we can help the young very far or deeply by all our teaching. Not only do they want their own experience, not ours, but it is right for them to have it. The urge of adolescence carries them away out of our detaining hands.

But that is not to say we are to push them into dangers. I believe we make the way too hard for the young with much of our nonsense about liberty and not interfering. You know what happens in a garden where the gardener does interfere with his hoe? I have been forced back, often reluctantly, into accepting the necessity of boundaries. I want right conduct to be defined, and defined widely with possible paths, so that the young may have a chance of finding their way.

We have, I am sure, to set up new conventions, establish fresh sanctions and accept prohibitions, to rebuild our broken ramparts and render safe and pleasant the city within. Do we fail to do this, we leave the young to stumble among the ruins we have made. And do not let us be hypocrites and profess surprise when they fall. The knowledge we are forcing on them, often against their desire, will not save them. With all our efforts we can but teach them intellectually; a form of knowledge, which shatters like thin glass, with a very slight blow, when it comes in contact with the emotions. Thus I am driven back to the truth, established already in an earlier essay, that the one sure way to deliver the young from evil is to lessen their temptations.

You see hidden sin is always more attractive than open sin; for one thing, it is easier to begin, and the beginning of sin is usually drifting; secrecy also supplies adventure, and the excitement that is desired by the young so passionately in the dullness of life.

C. Gasquoine Hartley

IV

There never was an age when so many diverse types of young women flourished, sometimes they are rather puzzling to the middle-aged observer.[200:1] With so many of them there is a kind of forced levity, a self-consciousness that prevents them from being either simple or serious. All the clever ones seem to think that by talking in generalizations, you can avert the plain issues of life. Their conversation is full of meaningless remarks, such as "the bondage of sex," "the superstition of chastity," "freedom in the marriage bond," "the sacrifice of women," "stifling convention," and so on, which they go on repeating because that is the terminology of their set. They have no conception of realities at all, only of abstract situations. Impossible to tell what are their pseudo-emotions; a sort of sterile intellectualism, shown in their shirking of sex responsibility. They wish to ignore the real difficulty of marriage; they accept love, but only with conditions. The one thing they face practically is work, and the two activities don't conflict in their estimates, because their minds are too choked with conceptions to admit facts. They are faithful to their training by G. Bernard Shaw and H. G. Wells, in thinking that by stating a situation and arguing about it, you can shirk the need of dealing with it.

Some women want to wipe the sex-side of life out. They cannot. They preach that work and human experience (whatever that may mean) will weaken sex-desire. It does not. Desires may be inhibited, not destroyed, corrupting in quietness they wait opportunity to revive, insistent, clamoring.

Other young women try deliberately to keep love light. Shrewd enough to understand the heavy claims of serious passion, they prefer affairs of the senses only; episodes that are a secret detachable part of their lives. They want love as an experience, and to provide the always desired excitement, but they want as well to remain free to take up other aspects of life. And while condescending to fascinate men while deliberately seeking attention, they still hold themselves in hand; intending to exploit life to the uttermost, they find sex amusing, but they fight always against its being a vocation.

There is, of course, a reason for this. The young are more reckless and lawless, they do more and go further than the last generation, and this is but an outward expression of disorder within, in my opinion, to be traced back to the passionate need felt by the young for love. So that whenever this love-desire is unsatisfied, or falsely satisfied, the dynamic need causes a kind of ferment, which sours love so that it becomes *desire to be considered*. If a woman is not important to others, she becomes important to herself, and this unconscious self-glorification is so devouring, so little based on anything that can possibly satisfy the need that is its cause, that it creates a hunger that can never be appeased, so constant are its demands for nourishment. It is difficult to say how far this insatiable egomania will take our young women. Some men are also empoisoned with it.

Both these types are modern; opposed to them is another type of young woman, more feminine, easier to explain, but also thwarted, restlessly demanding an outlet. These women do not want to furl their sex, they seek lovers to whom they may surrender themselves, but they suffer from a formless discontent that rots into every love and prevents them finding satisfaction. Eternally they are unsatisfied, without knowing why.

It is another modern disease and has little connection with flirting and lightness of character, though often the two are confused. Too restless to be faithful, born spiritual

C. Gasquoine Hartley

adventurers, these worshipers of emotionalism set up elaborate pretenses of pure friendships, ignoring the hot glow within: they love romantically, but rarely are strong enough to obey their inclinations. Such women are out on an eternal quest, and every now and again, they believe they have found what they are seeking. Then they discover they have not found it, so their search is taken up anew; while often the social scheme drives them into dangerous corners, forces them to turn from their quest or to use mean weapons of deceit, does not give them a chance.

These romantic seekers of love, suffering continual frustration from the evaporation of emotional interest that defies their own needs; the many types of efficient workers, alert, hard, self-satisfied, not wholly cynical, yet with a touch of something that borders on cynicism, submitting almost with a secret repugnance to the mysterious but supreme bond which holds the sexes miserably together; and the prostitute woman of all kinds, out to seize every advantage from men, ruthless, living upon sex—these are, it seems to me, the three main types of women resulting in our so-called civilization of to-day, from our repressions and falsehoods, our indefinite wills, from our confused ideals and failure in living; and it is hard to say which is the most harmful, which is the most wronged, which is the most unhappy, the furthest removed from the type that is eternal—the ideal woman, satisfied and glad, whom a happier future may again permit to live.

V

It was Mr. Wells who said in one of his novels, "suppose the liberation of women simply means the liberation of mischief." "Suppose she *is* wicked as a sex, suppose she *will* trade on her power of exciting imaginative men."

Something very like this has been happening in the world to-day.

We are all to pieces morally. The consciences of many people are their neighbor's opinions, and the removal of so many young girls and men from their home surroundings, their relations and old friends, has greatly slackened the watchful safe-guarding of morals, so that any slightest infringement has not been at once observed and quickly punished. The important barriers of difference in class, in social positions, and in race have also broken through. Conditions in the five war-years and most of the arrangements of society have discouraged morality very heavily, and the wise thing for us to do in the matter is not to grow eloquent about sin, but at once to do intelligent things to make right conduct easier.

An organized freedom and independence for women has certainly had startling moral results. The reasons are obvious enough. It is a necessary consequence of our modern insistence on individual values; the harping of one generation on freedom, which has caused our young women, in many directions, to carry their ideas of freedom far beyond the accepted conventions of our ordinary civilized human association. It has been shown as manifestly true that for all ordinary young women that intimate association with men, fellowship in the workshops and factories and in play, turns them with extreme readiness to love-making. Now, I

C. Gasquoine Hartley

am very far from wishing to blame women; rather am I glad that what I have asserted, for so long and against so much opposition, about the elementary power of sex in women, has been vindicated by themselves.

Life for women so often has been wrong and discordant, and the wretchedness has been greatly increased by the way we have left, in the immediate past, the force of sex unregulated and unrecognized, thereby causing much of the modern companionship of women with men, of girls with boys, to be really a monstrous sham, maintained and made exciting by false situations that often have closed around the two like a trap.

There are, and always have been, far more women and girls than we like to acknowledge who are by their inclinations sexually promiscuous. It is just conventional rot to talk of sex impulse being weaker and quite different in women from men; of constancy as the special virtue of women. Sometimes it is, but oftener it is not. It depends on the type of woman. A great and possibly increasing number of girls today regard love affairs in very much the same way as they are regarded by the average sensual man, as enjoyable and exciting incidents of which they are ashamed only when they are talked about and blamed. Such girls very rarely give trouble to men or make scenes, they don't care enough; that, I think, is why they always find lovers. It is also why it is easy for them to have secret relations. With no sex-conscience, such girls, even when quite young, exhibit a logic and a frankness that sometimes is rather startling. They seem to have no modesty, though many of them are prudes; they have no consciousness of responsibility; they feel no kind of shame. Such libidinous temperaments have been common at all times and in all societies, if in stricter periods so many women did not follow their inclinations with the openness now so frequent, it was simply out of fear; possibly they took more careful precautions against discovery.

There are as well as these wantons, girls of a different type, who are more contradictory and difficult because of a less simple sexuality, but who are equally, even if not more, harmfully destructive in the utter misery they often create. This is the type of girl who ripens to a premature and too emotional sexuality, and who, though still keeping herself physically intact, is spiritually corrupt. The spiritual masochism of a woman may lead to depths of cruelty rarely understood.[208:1]

Many other nobler types of women have been playing with vice. Many wild impulses have found strange expressions. Women have been very like children playing at desperate rebels, who take up weapons to use far more deadly than they knew. All this playing with love is detestable, all of it. It shows a shameful shirking of responsibility. Women are the custodians of manners in love, and very many, who have not dreamt of the results of their slackenings, have been urging on the young to a riotous festival, extravagant and disquieting.

It must, I think, be acknowledged that a vast impatience on the part of women has made conduct less decent and less responsible. Lovers are more reckless, even sometimes more consciously and vulgarly vicious. Women of profound and steadfast emotional nature are rare. The great majority now, perhaps, are not entirely light-minded, but they are less serious, more noisily determined to do what they want, and get what they can both out of men and out of life.

And the great fact that stands out from all this—the great need for our private personal good as well as the public good—is the need of the young for guidance and regulation, the necessity for refixing of moral standards in sexual conduct, of formulating a code of good manners, to meet the present needs. Nothing else, in my opinion, can avert even greater disasters of license in the future, than those conditions we are now facing.

VI

New wine is being put into old bottles and the wine of life is being poured out and wasted. The old convention that irregular love is excusable in the case of the man, but always to be punished in the case of the woman will never again be accepted, at least not by women. It is not women's ideas so much that are confused as their emotions, and wills. Their impulses are not focused to any ideal. They are driven hither and thither. That is the essential failure to-day. The irregular unions, now so common, are but the more intimate aspect of a general attitude toward life. Many women who have entered them, have done so rather in a mood of protesting refractoriness than from any serviceable desire; already they find themselves left after transitory passionate friendships in difficult situations in which there is as yet no certain tradition of behavior. And in this way, there is left open an inviting door to those who are weak, as well as to those who are corrupt, to behave irresponsibly and commit every kind of uncleanness.

Where is this wild love going to end?

These dissatisfied women of strong sexuality, and women of the other types I have noted, must either marry or must continue lawless careers of unregulated promiscuity, each one acting according to her own fancy, curbed only by the will of her lover or lovers, and the circumstances in which she is placed: there is at present no third course.

Now, the moralist, who does not face facts, would have them all marry. Certainly this is an easy way to settle the matter, but is it wise? is it even right? Moreover, even if this were possible and there was no surplus of women, would this solution be acceptable to these women? I am doubtful if it would. *Many of them who want a lover do not want a husband*, they make a surprisingly clear distinction between the two. There is, as I have before said, a hardly-yet-realized change in woman's attitude: they are beginning to take the ordinary man's view of these affairs,—to regard them as important and providing interest and pleasure, but not to be exaggerated into tragedies. They deliberately want to keep love light and dread the bondage of any deep emotions.

Now, such an attitude is not good for marriage, and, indeed, there can be no manner of use in forcing into the marriage bonds those who are unwilling to accept its duties of permanent devotion. Some other way, more practical and more helpful, must be found. We shall have, I am convinced, to broaden our views on this question of passionate friendships between women and men, to reconsider the whole position of sexual relationships apart from marriage, in order to decide what may be permitted, to regulate conduct and fasten responsibility, to open up in the future new ways of virtue. And in attempting, thus, to face squarely the difficult situations before us, I can find only one clear simple and honest way to act.

VII

We come, then, to this: how can the way be made plainer for those women and also men who are unsuited for marriage and do not wish to devote their lives to its duties?

I believe that if there were some open recognition of honorable partnerships outside of marriage, not necessarily permanent, with proper provision for the future, guarding the woman, who, in my opinion, should be in all cases protected; a provision not dependent on the generosity of the man and made after the love which sanctioned the union has waned, but decided upon by the man and the woman in the form of a registered contract before the relationship was entered upon, then there would everywhere be women ready to undertake such unions gladly, there would, indeed, be many women, as well as men, who, for the reasons I have shown, would prefer them to marriage.

There is (I must again insist upon this), whether we like it or not, a new kind of woman about, who is to snatch from life the freedom that men have had, and to do this, she knows, if she thinks at all, that she must keep marriage at bay. For marriage binds the woman while it frees the man, and this injustice—if so you like to term it—is dependent on something fundamental; something that will not be changed by endowment of motherhood, an equal moral standard in the marriage laws, or any of the modern patent medicines for giving health to marriage and liberty to wives. There is an inescapable difference in the results of marriage on the two partners. I mean, marriage holds the woman bound through her emotions, while it liberates the man through what he receives from her. The woman gains her greatest liberation only from the child, but again that holds her bound. Perhaps this is the way nature will not let women get away from their

C. Gasquoine Hartley

service to life.

Sometimes there is the necessity of purifying by loss. I do not believe in changing the ideal of marriage so that its duties are less binding on women, already we have gone too far in that direction. Thus, I think it better to make provision for other partnerships to meet the sex-needs (for we can cause nothing but evil by failing to meet them) of those women who, desiring the same freedom as the man, would delegate the duties of wife and mother to the odd moments of life, and choose to pursue work or pleasure unvexed and unimpeded by the home duties and care of children. Marriage also is a trust; we are the trustees to the future for the most sacred institution of life.

VIII

A society parched for honesty cannot suffer the ignominious and chaotic conditions of our sexual lives to go on as they have been lately among us, for it is plain to me that our moral code—that marriage itself cannot stand, and, indeed, is not standing, the strain of our dishonesties. Our social life is worm-eaten and crumbling into rottenness with secret and scandalous hidden relationships; these dark and musty by-ways and corners of sexual conduct want to be spring-cleaned and made decent. Never before have we needed so urgently to put our house in order. We must begin to tidy up and begin soon. If we cut out some parts of the labyrinth, we shall give the young a surer chance of finding their way out of the rest of the labyrinth.

C. Gasquoine Hartley

IX

An open recognition of unions outside of marriage would prevent the present easy escape on the part of so many men and women from responsible conduct in these unregulated relationships. It is because I believe this that I am advocating this course, which will not make immorality easier, but rather will impose definite obligations where now none exist.

This proposal is not made lightly. I am not advocating such a course as being in itself desirable or undesirable. I am attempting merely to estimate the drift and tendency of the times, considering those forces which for long have been in action and, as I think, must continue to act with even greater urgency in the difficult years that are before us.

I must affirm how necessary, in my opinion, is some kind of fixed recognition for every form of sexual relationship between a woman and a man, so that there may be an accepted standard of conduct for the partners entering into them. Regulation is more necessary in sex than in any other department of conduct, for the plain reason that we are dealing with a force that pierces the slashes through our conscious wills, holding us often helpless in its power; a force which often finds its momentum in atavisms stored up through countless ages before ever society began; a force merely glossed over, as it were, by a worn smudge of civilization. And to-day "the smudge" has grown more than ever ineffective.

May not something be done now, when we are being forced to consider these questions, to make some wider recognition possible. Partnerships other than marriage have had a place as a recognized and guarded institution in many older, and in some ways wiser, societies, and, it may be that the conditions brought upon us after the World War may act in forcing upon us a similar acceptance. I believe that, in face of much that is happening to-day—the terrible disorder, like spreading-sores, infesting our sexual lives—such a change would work for good, and not for evil, that it would not destroy marriage, but might re-establish its sanctity.

C. Gasquoine Hartley

X

I can anticipate an objection that probably will be raised. Why, I shall be asked, if sexual relationships are to be acknowledged outside of marriage, preserve marriages at all? This question can be answered confidently. Marriage in its permanent monogamous form will be maintained because the great majority of women and men want it to be maintained. The contract-partnerships I have suggested will be powerless to harm wedded love, of which the child is the glorious symbol. No law is needed to protect this beauty. There will always remain a penalty to those who seek variety in love, in that unrest that is the other side of variety.

It is the highest type of men and women who will seek to marry and be best and happiest, if living together as faithful husband and wife, as devoted father and mother, I do, however, hold, that there are others—women and men—without the gifts that make for successful parenthood or happy permanent marriage. I would recognize this frankly, and let those who do not desire marriage be openly permitted to live together in honorable temporary unions.

Surely it is the wisest arrangement for the man and woman worker who do not want children, and, not wishing for the bondage of a continuous companionship, desire to pass their lives in liberty. It is possible that in some cases such friendship-contracts might serve as a preliminary to marriage, while, under our present disastrous conditions, they might also be made by those who are unsuitably mated and yet are unable, or do not wish, to sever the bond with some other partner. Such contracts would open up possibilities of honorable relations to many who now are driven into shameful and secret unions.

In this way much evil would be prevented. As time went on, hasty marriage would come to be looked on with disapproval, and many unions would be prevented that now inevitably come to disaster. And this would leave greater chances of marriage and child-bearing for others and more suitable types; while further, these sterile unions would, by their childlessness, act to remove for ever from the world those unsuited to be parents. It is this last result that matters most.

C. Gasquoine Hartley

XI

The whole question of any sexual relationships outside of marriage in the past has been left in the gutters, so to speak, of necessity made disreputable by the shames of concealment. Much of this would be changed. Moreover, prostitution, and also the diseases so closely connected with prostitution, would be greatly lessened, though I do not think sexual sins would cease. There will always be, for a very long time at least, men and women who will be attracted to wild-love. This we have to recognize. No one, however, need be driven into the dark paths of irresponsible love.

It is the results that have almost always followed these irregular unions that have always branded them as anti-social acts. But irresponsible conduct, such, for instance, as the desertion of women, which is made easy by the condition of secrecy under which they now exist, would be put an end to. And by doing this would follow another and, perhaps, even greater gain. The recognition of these partnerships would prevent the ostracism which even yet falls on the discarded mistress. There are many women who dread this more than anything else. A woman is hounded out of decent life, if the facts of her history become known; honorable love is closed to her, too often she finds the easiest and pleasantest life is that of the streets.

One reason why extra-conjugal relationships are discredited is, because the difficulties placed around all who enter them are so numerous that, as a rule, it is the weak, the foolish and the irresponsible who undertake these partnerships. Of course, this is not always true. Men and women, against their wills and often before they know, become entangled in a net of furtive and dishonorable acts. Squalid intrigues are the shadow that I want to eliminate out of existence. But make these partnerships honorable, and the men and women who enter into them will act honorably. I do not see that we can forbid or treat with bitterness any union that is openly entered into and in which the duties undertaken are faithfully fulfilled. It is our attitude of blame that so often makes decent conduct impossible; forces men and women into corners where there is no escape from embittered rebellious sin.

C. Gasquoine Hartley

XII

I have sought to put these matters as plainly as may be in the conviction that nothing can be gained without honesty. Anyone who writes on such a question is, I know, very open to misconception. It will not be realized by many that my effort is not to lessen responsibility,—to weaken at all the bonds between the sexes, rather my desire is to strengthen them; but, I know, the form of the bonds will have to be made wider. We shall have more morality in too much wideness than in too little.

Matters are likely to get worse and not better. And the answer I would give to those who fear an increase of immorality from any openly recognized provision for sexual partnerships outside of permanent marriage is that no deliberate change made in this direction can conceivably make the moral conditions of our society, in the future, worse than they have been in the recent past. As a matter of fact, every form of irregular union has existed and does exist to-day, but shamefully and hidden. It is certain that they will continue and that their numbers will not lessen, but increase.

The only logical objection that I can think of being advanced against an honorable recognition of these partnerships is that, by doing away with all necessity for concealments, their number is likely to be much larger than if the old penalties were maintained. I doubt if this would happen, but, even if it were so, and more of these partnerships were entered into; it is also true that recognition is the only possible way in which such union can cease to be shameful. We have, then, to choose whether we will accept recognition and regulations, unless, indeed, we prefer the continuance and increase of unregulated secret vice.

There is no other choice, at least I can find none; no other way except to establish responsibility in all our sexual relationships. Secret relationships must be contraband in the new order.

FOOTNOTES:

[193:1] Some parts of this essay appeared, in 1913, in the *English Review*. The article created some interest at that time, especially in America, where it was published (with two other articles from the *English Review*) in a little book, "Women and Morality." My opinions have changed little since I wrote it. In my last book, "Motherhood and the Relationships of the Sexes," I again treat the subject in a chapter entitled *Sexual Relationships outside of Marriage*. I am now strengthened in my certainty that responsibility must be fixed and regulated in all sexual relationships if moral health is to be restored.

[200:1] A clever novel, "Three Women," by Miss Netta Syrett, gives an illuminating picture of modern womanhood.

[208:1] See I. Bloch, "Sexual History of our Times," pp. 320-322.

CONCLUSION

WITHOUT VISION

"Where there is no vision, the people perish."—Pro. xxix. 18.

I began this book on Armistice day, and am ending it on Peace day. This period of about eight months has been a time of great disillusionment. Even those little inclined to be deceived by the customary exaggerations of politicians, and little disposed to believe in sudden conversions, had hoped that the immense effort of this Great War was to awaken the deadened conscience of the world; to leave a permanent improvement in social and international relations; making class and individual and sex competition, as also national rivalry, a less pronounced feature in the new order; replacing greed by desire for service, war by a League of Nations to enforce justice. But a war of justice was followed by a peace of trickery and injustice. The victors (if not every one of them, still collectively) claimed their spoils as in earlier wars. Clemenceau's desire for vengeance triumphed over Wilson's principles in the center of the world stage.

More than ever we search the future with anxiety. Amid the confusions and compulsions, the changes unavoidable in this time of uncertainty, it is immensely more difficult to act wisely. In the old days it all seemed so much easier, as if life could be shuffled, like a pack of cards, into new arrangements. War has made a difference to the whole of life, shattered everything, as it were, in our hands, made the daily duties of most of us much harder. We have been robbed of serenity.

When you stand at the threshold of this new difficult world, knowing, as I do, that the milestones marking the backward path tell you, with certainty, that the greater part of your life and your work lies behind you, then, in these waiting days of urgency, you will want to hold a reckoning with yourself and with life, in humility to question everything, your own faith and what you have tried to teach to others with all the honesty you have.

My task has been a difficult one, and it is made much more difficult by reason of the uncertainties of our outlook, because there are now so few principles accepted by all of us as true; every principle is faced by a counter principle. It is so much easier to have fixed standards of conduct than to argue every case that occurs. We have failed in every direction to establish ideals fine enough and complete enough, and useful enough to hold our imagination and our wills. Everyone seems to be more or less at loose ends of conflicting purposes. Morals now are like clothes, made to measure and to fit each wearer. Too often, in important particulars, they change as easily and foolishly as the fashions change.

I wish to bring people back to a disciplined freedom; to a recognition of their own needs and the needs of others—the deepest desires of life. A morality based on individual values is breaking down in every direction, under the temptations and unsettlements, increased and hastened by the war, but

C. Gasquoine Hartley

brought about primarily by profit seeking, by the struggle of everyone doing as he likes, by a society so large, so ill organized and so hurried that personal intercourse gives way to mechanical relationships.

My position is all the more difficult as, while inclining more to the spirit of those who, in relation to the moral questions I have dealt with, are conservative, I yet regard very many of our accepted conventions and our laws as productive of evil. I realize the way in which they act so disastrously in hindering the spiritual and physical health of our society. I am, therefore, eager for certain very wide-reaching reforms.

I have not great patience with abstract theories of right and wrong, rather I would test every law and every institution by its usefulness in helping men and women. However imperfectly I have succeeded, I have set *this aim of helpfulness* steadfastly before me in every proposal I have made for changes in our marriage laws and in the hindering laws which regulate personal conduct. I do not want to discuss and consider humanity, life, or anything else as I would like them to be, but, as honestly as I can, I would observe and then help them as they are.

So many calamities and so much sin that could be prevented are listlessly accepted by us as inevitable. New ideas and needs are entangled among old; there is much of the new that is desirable to preserve, much of the old that needs to be reformed. I would wish to oppose two tendencies: I would prevent the too ready acceptance of the fashions of the day, and I would also prevent a too loyal obedience to the prejudices of yesterday. I would unite the intelligence of the modern with the passion and sincerity of the ancient.

Such is the immensely difficult task that must be faced by every one of us to-day. All of us are charged with heavy responsibility. Ours is a greater inheritance than ever before there has been in the world. We have all of us become responsible in a new and sterner way; to unite in our search to find the new right paths. Three generations of industrialism have created hideous abuses; we have to end them. With our wider vision and more knowledge, with the lessons we have learned, with the pain of our suffering, and our sacrifices still branded on our hearts, we have to unite one with the other and all of us together to renew and to justify life. We have to remake the world.

C. Gasquoine Hartley

APPENDIX I

TABLE 1.—Summary of the Position as regards the Employment of Women, April, 1914.

OCCUPATION	Estimated Number of Women employed, July, 1914.	Percentage of Women to Total Number of Workpeople employed, July, 1914.	Increase in the Employment of Women since July, 1914	
			Percentage of these employed in July, 1918.	Approximate Increase in Numbers.
Industries	2,176,000	26	25	537,000
Government Establishments	2,000	3	9,098	197,000
Gas, Water, Electricity (under Local Authorities)	600	1	724	4,000
Agriculture	80,000	9	11	9,000
Transport	17,000	2	459	78,000
Tramways	1,200	2	1,466	18,000
Finance and Banking	9,300	5	660	63,000
Commerce	296,000	29	71	354,000
Professions (mainly Clerks)	50,500	28	118	57,000
Hotels, Public Houses, Cinemas, Theaters, etc.	181,000	48	14	25,000
Civil Service, Post Office	60,300	24	78	59,500
Other Civil Service	5,500	9	1,809	99,500
Other Services under Local Authorities	196,200	34	16	31,000
Total	**3,276,000**	**24**	**47**	**1,532,000**

OCCUPATION	Numbers of Women stated by Employers to be directly replacing Men.	Percentage of Women to Total Number of Workpeople employed, April, 1918.
Industries	531,000	36
Government Establishments	187,000	44
Gas, Water, Electricity (under Local Authorities)	4,000	9
Agriculture	40,000	13
Transport	79,000	10
Tramways	17,000	34
Finance and Banking	59,000	40
Commerce	352,000	53
Professions (mainly Clerks)	22,000	61
Hotels, Public Houses, Cinemas, Theaters, etc.	44,500	61
Civil Service, Post Office	64,000	52
Other Civil Service	89,000	57
Other Services under Local Authorities	26,000	47
Total	1,516,000	37

C. Gasquoine Hartley

TABLE II.— The Employment of Women in the Main Groups of Industrial Occupations, April 1916, 1917, 1918.

OCCUPATIONS	Estimated number of Women employed July, 1914.	Increase (+), Decrease (-),since July 1914, in the number of Women employed.			Women stated by Employers to be replacing Men, April 1916.
		April 1916	April 1917	April 1918	
Metal Trades	170,000	+149,200	+295,300	+385,000	194,000
Chemical Trades	40,000	+34,300	+66,000	+63,000	81,000
Textile Trades	863,000	+19,200	+14,500	-19,000	65,000
Clothing Trades	612,000	+12,800	-44,700	-37,000	46,000
Food Trades	196,000	+17,100	+25,000	+30,000	62,000
Paper and Printing Trades	147,000	-700	-5,100	-4,000	21,000
Wood Trades	44,000	+14,000	+21,000	+34,000	26,000
All Industrial Occupations, including some not specified above	2,176,000	+284,000	+483,000	+537,000	510,000

TABLE III.— Analysis of Pre-War Occupation of Women made by Special Inquiry, January 1917.

PRE-WAR OCCUPATION

Present Occupation.	Same Occupation.	Household Duties, and not previously occupied.	Textile Trades.	Clothing Trades.
Metal Trades	53,249	18,927	3,408	4,635
Chemical Trades	14,634	52,407	6,226	17,941
Textile Trades	6,378	4,730	1,377	3,695
Clothing Trades	38,256	9,334	1,000	8,430
Wood Trades	4,439	3,764	783	1,490
Leather Trades	7,682	2,179	695	1,372
Rubber Trades	7,897	4,055	1,119	1,561
Others	4,003	3,115	400	669
Total	136,538	98,511	15,008	39,793

Present Occupation.	Other Industries.	Domestic Service.	Other Industrial Occupations.	Total stated and classified.
Metal Trades	12,458	12,502	5,449	110,628
Chemical Trades	20,879	44,438	17,079	173,604
Textile Trades	2,320	2,531	1,054	22,085
Clothing Trades	5,745	4,970	3,643	71,378
Wood Trades	2,626	3,950	1,196	18,248
Leather Trades	1,782	1,311	822	15,843
Rubber Trades	2,104	2,393	1,030	20,159
Others	1,233	1,897	875	12,192
Total	49,147	73,992	31,148	444,137

C. Gasquoine Hartley

TABLE IV.— Showing Changes between July, 1914, and October, 1918, in Numbers of Girls under 18 employed in Various Occupations.

| OCCUPATIONS WITH-- | Numbers on | | Gross | |
	July 1914.	Oct. 1918.	Increase.	Decrease.
(1) *Very large Increase.*				
Building and Construction	1,500	6,000	4,500	...
Metal Trades	45,000	108,000	63,000	...
Chemical Trades	11,000	25,000	14,000	...
Woodworking Trades	10,500	20,000	9,500	...
Other Trades	26,000	37,000	11,000	...
Total in Industry	94,000	196,000	102,000	...
(2) *Large Increase, but no serious problem.*				
Mines and Quarries	1,500	4,000	2,500	...
Agriculture	12,000	18,000	6,000	...
Professional Occupations	5,000	11,000	6,000	...
Postal Service	10,000	14,000	4,000	...
Municipal Gas, Water, and Electricity	...	1,000	1,000	...
Municipal Tramways	...	1,000	1,000	...
Other Local Government Service	5,000	8,000	3,000	...
Total in Class 2	33,500	57,000	23,500	...
(3) *Small Increase.*				
Food, Drink, and Tobacco Trades	49,000	53,000	4,000	...

TABLE V.— Number of Children and Young Persons convicted of Indictable Offenses in Juvenile Courts in large Cities and in the Metropolitan Police Area from 1914-1917.

INDICTABLE OFFENSES.	1914	1915	1916	1917
Manchester	435	708	767	750
Liverpool	1,169	1,545	2,013	2,196
Leeds	191	256	295	385
Bristol	106	207	331	279
Birmingham	368	423	504	625
Newcastle	86	177	222	234
	2,355	3,316	4,132	4,469
Metropolitan Police District	1,778	3,069	3,858	3,856

C. Gasquoine Hartley

APPENDIX II

SOME STATISTICS REFERRING TO THE ILLEGITIMATELY BORN CHILD.

1. Births.

About 50,000 illegitimate children are born yearly in the United Kingdom. Consider what this means. In the course of a single generation of twenty years one million of these unprotected little ones are born, branded because their parents have acted illegitimately.[235:1]

The exact figures for England and Wales[235:2] during the past five and a half years are as follows:

Year	Total Births	Legitimate	Illegitimate	Illegitimate Percentage Total
1913	881,890	848,981	37,909	4.29
1914	879,096	841,767	37,329	4.24
1915	814,614	778,369	36,245	4.44
1916	785,520	747,831	37,689	4.79
1917	668,346	631,336	37,010	5.54
1918[235:3]	332,547	312,587	19,960	6.0

It should be noted that in England still-born births are not registered; were these recorded the illegitimate birth-rate would be much higher than the present statistics show. In those countries where the records are kept the number of still-born illegitimate births is always very high, sometimes twice as high—as it is for children born under the protection of marriage.

2. Deaths.

An unusually high infant mortality is found everywhere among illegitimate children. In general, the illegitimate rate is twice as great as the legitimate. *Two unprotected children die for each protected child.*

1912-1916 DEATHS PER 1,000 UNDER 1 YEAR.

	All infants under 1 year.	Legitimate.	Illegitimate.
1912	95	91	121
1913	106	104	213
1914	105	100	207
1915	190	105	203
1916	91	87	183

The mortality of unmarried mothers is proportionately great.

"The ratio of illegitimate to legitimate mortality in the first week of life has increased from 170 per cent. in 1907 to 201 per cent. in 1916. These facts have a somewhat ominous aspect and suggest that infant welfare organizations might

C. Gasquoine Hartley

well devote special attention to the first days of the life of illegitimate children."—(*Report of the Registrar-General for 1916.*)

The Law of Affiliation and Bastardy. (Brief Summary of the Law in England and Wales.)

The mother is the legal parent. The child is not legitimized on the marriage of its parents. The child has no rights of inheritance from either parent. Where paternity is established the father is liable for support (or alimony). In Scotland the marriage of the mother with the father legitimizes the child. In Ireland the mother is not allowed to claim alimony herself—she must go into the workhouse and the guardians must sue for her.

To Obtain an Affiliation Order.

By the Bastardy Laws Amendment Act, 1872, the mother must apply to a justice of the peace for a summons to be served on the man alleged by her to be the father of her child. The cost of this summons is 3/6 with an additional 2/- for delivery if beyond the limits of a city borough. The cost of the affiliation order, when obtained, is 9/-. The application for the order may be made before the birth of the child or within twelve months after the birth. It cannot be done after that time unless (1) the man has acknowledged his paternity by paying money for the child, (2) the alleged father has left England, in which case a summons can be served any time within 12 months after his return.

The Affiliation Order.

The maximum amount that up to the present time has been allowed under an Affiliation Order is 5/- a week, such payments to continue until the child reaches the age of sixteen years. The justices determine the exact amount the father shall pay. It also rests entirely within their discretion to make any allowance for the mother's expenses at the time of birth. In fixing the sum the justices are supposed to act *having regard to all the circumstances of the case*, and often the payments were fixed as low as 2/6 or 3/6 per week before the passing of New Act 1919.

The Affiliation Orders Act, 1914.

By the Affiliation Orders Act, 1914, two important changes in the law were gained. The appointment of an officer, known as the collecting officer, took out of the hands of the mother the work of collecting the weekly payments granted under the maintenance order, while new powers were given of enforcing payment from a defaulting father. Further, the compulsory interval of six days (a period which gave the man opportunity to escape) between the summons and the appearance in court of the putative father was abolished.

The New Act.

The inadequacy of such sums with which to bring up a child has at last led to action, and the maximum of 5/- a week has been done away with. The maximum payment in the future will be 10/- a week. This Act (which is called the Affiliation Orders Increase of Maximum Payment Act, 1918) came into operation on January 1st, 1919.

C. Gasquoine Hartley

Provisions Affecting Soldiers and Sailors.

If a soldier is alleged to be the father of the child, action must be taken while he is in England or Wales. In Scotland and Ireland the bastardy laws are different, and if he is abroad or under orders to go abroad action cannot be taken. The summons should be served on his commanding officer, with a sufficient payment to cover his journey to and from the court where his case is to be heard. Before the war the alimony granted to the mother for a child by a soldier was even less than in ordinary cases; this injustice has, however, been ended and the allowance now granted for an illegitimate child is 6/8 per week.

FOOTNOTES

[235:1] The word illegitimacy is derived from the Latin *illegitimus*, meaning "not in accordance with law."

[235:2] The bastardy laws in Scotland and Ireland are different from the English laws, and therefore the figures for these countries are not given.

[235:3] First half-year.

Choose from Thousands of 1stWorldLibrary Classics By

A. M. Barnard
Ada Leverson
Adolphus William Ward
Aesop
Agatha Christie
Alexander Aaronsohn
Alexander Kielland
Alexandre Dumas
Alfred Gatty
Alfred Ollivant
Alice Duer Miller
Alice Turner Curtis
Alice Dunbar
Allen Chapman
Alleyne Ireland
Ambrose Bierce
Amelia E. Barr
Amory H. Bradford
Andrew Lang
Andrew McFarland Davis
Andy Adams
Angela Brazil
Anna Alice Chapin
Anna Sewell
Annie Besant
Annie Hamilton Donnell
Annie Payson Call
Annie Roe Carr
Annonaymous
Anton Chekhov
Archibald Lee Fletcher
Arnold Bennett
Arthur C. Benson
Arthur Conan Doyle
Arthur M. Winfield
Arthur Ransome
Arthur Schnitzler
Arthur Train
Atticus
B.H. Baden-Powell
B. M. Bower
B. C. Chatterjee
Baroness Emmuska Orczy
Baroness Orczy
Basil King
Bayard Taylor
Ben Macomber
Bertha Muzzy Bower
Bjornstjerne Bjornson

Booth Tarkington
Boyd Cable
Bram Stoker
C. Collodi
C. E. Orr
C. M. Ingleby
Carolyn Wells
Catherine Parr Traill
Charles A. Eastman
Charles Amory Beach
Charles Dickens
Charles Dudley Warner
Charles Farrar Browne
Charles Ives
Charles Kingsley
Charles Klein
Charles Hanson Towne
Charles Lathrop Pack
Charles Romyn Dake
Charles Whibley
Charles Willing Beale
Charlotte M. Braeme
Charlotte M. Yonge
Charlotte Perkins Stetson
Clair W. Hayes
Clarence Day Jr.
Clarence E. Mulford
Clemence Housman
Confucius
Coningsby Dawson
Cornelis DeWitt Wilcox
Cyril Burleigh
D. H. Lawrence
Daniel Defoe
David Garnett
Dinah Craik
Don Carlos Janes
Donald Keyhoe
Dorothy Kilner
Dougan Clark
Douglas Fairbanks
E. Nesbit
E. P. Roe
E. Phillips Oppenheim
E. S. Brooks
Earl Barnes
Edgar Rice Burroughs
Edith Van Dyne
Edith Wharton

Edward Everett Hale
Edward J. O'Biren
Edward S. Ellis
Edwin L. Arnold
Eleanor Atkins
Eleanor Hallowell Abbott
Eliot Gregory
Elizabeth Gaskell
Elizabeth McCracken
Elizabeth Von Arnim
Ellem Key
Emerson Hough
Emilie F. Carlen
Emily Bronte
Emily Dickinson
Enid Bagnold
Enilor Macartney Lane
Erasmus W. Jones
Ernie Howard Pie
Ethel May Dell
Ethel Turner
Ethel Watts Mumford
Eugene Sue
Eugenie Foa
Eugene Wood
Eustace Hale Ball
Evelyn Everett-green
Everard Cotes
F. H. Cheley
F. J. Cross
F. Marion Crawford
Fannie E. Newberry
Federick Austin Ogg
Ferdinand Ossendowski
Fergus Hume
Florence A. Kilpatrick
Fremont B. Deering
Francis Bacon
Francis Darwin
Frances Hodgson Burnett
Frances Parkinson Keyes
Frank Gee Patchin
Frank Harris
Frank Jewett Mather
Frank L. Packard
Frank V. Webster
Frederic Stewart Isham
Frederick Trevor Hill
Frederick Winslow Taylor

Friedrich Kerst
Friedrich Nietzsche
Fyodor Dostoyevsky
G.A. Henty
G.K. Chesterton
Gabrielle E. Jackson
Garrett P. Serviss
Gaston Leroux
George A. Warren
George Ade
Geroge Bernard Shaw
George Cary Eggleston
George Durston
George Ebers
George Eliot
George Gissing
George MacDonald
George Meredith
George Orwell
George Sylvester Viereck
George Tucker
George W. Cable
George Wharton James
Gertrude Atherton
Gordon Casserly
Grace E. King
Grace Gallatin
Grace Greenwood
Grant Allen
Guillermo A. Sherwell
Gulielma Zollinger
Gustav Flaubert
H. A. Cody
H. B. Irving
H.C. Bailey
H. G. Wells
H. H. Munro
H. Irving Hancock
H. R. Naylor
H. Rider Haggard
H. W. C. Davis
Haldeman Julius
Hall Caine
Hamilton Wright Mabie
Hans Christian Andersen
Harold Avery
Harold McGrath
Harriet Beecher Stowe
Harry Castlemon
Harry Coghill
Harry Houidini

Hayden Carruth
Helent Hunt Jackson
Helen Nicolay
Hendrik Conscience
Hendy David Thoreau
Henri Barbusse
Henrik Ibsen
Henry Adams
Henry Ford
Henry Frost
Henry James
Henry Jones Ford
Henry Seton Merriman
Henry W Longfellow
Herbert A. Giles
Herbert Carter
Herbert N. Casson
Herman Hesse
Hildegard G. Frey
Homer
Honore De Balzac
Horace B. Day
Horace Walpole
Horatio Alger Jr.
Howard Pyle
Howard R. Garis
Hugh Lofting
Hugh Walpole
Humphry Ward
Ian Maclaren
Inez Haynes Gillmore
Irving Bacheller
Isabel Cecilia Williams
Isabel Hornibrook
Israel Abrahams
Ivan Turgenev
J.G.Austin
J. Henri Fabre
J. M. Barrie
J. M. Walsh
J. Macdonald Oxley
J. R. Miller
J. S. Fletcher
J. S. Knowles
J. Storer Clouston
J. W. Duffield
Jack London
Jacob Abbott
James Allen
James Andrews
James Baldwin

James Branch Cabell
James DeMille
James Joyce
James Lane Allen
James Lane Allen
James Oliver Curwood
James Oppenheim
James Otis
James R. Driscoll
Jane Abbott
Jane Austen
Jane L. Stewart
Janet Aldridge
Jens Peter Jacobsen
Jerome K. Jerome
Jessie Graham Flower
John Buchan
John Burroughs
John Cournos
John F. Kennedy
John Gay
John Glasworthy
John Habberton
John Joy Bell
John Kendrick Bangs
John Milton
John Philip Sousa
John Taintor Foote
Jonas Lauritz Idemil Lie
Jonathan Swift
Joseph A. Altsheler
Joseph Carey
Joseph Conrad
Joseph E. Badger Jr
Joseph Hergesheimer
Joseph Jacobs
Jules Vernes
Julian Hawthrone
Julie A Lippmann
Justin Huntly McCarthy
Kakuzo Okakura
Karle Wilson Baker
Kate Chopin
Kenneth Grahame
Kenneth McGaffey
Kate Langley Bosher
Kate Langley Bosher
Katherine Cecil Thurston
Katherine Stokes
L. A. Abbot
L. T. Meade

L. Frank Baum
Latta Griswold
Laura Dent Crane
Laura Lee Hope
Laurence Housman
Lawrence Beasley
Leo Tolstoy
Leonid Andreyev
Lewis Carroll
Lewis Sperry Chafer
Lilian Bell
Lloyd Osbourne
Louis Hughes
Louis Joseph Vance
Louis Tracy
Louisa May Alcott
Lucy Fitch Perkins
Lucy Maud Montgomery
Luther Benson
Lydia Miller Middleton
Lyndon Orr
M. Corvus
M. H. Adams
Margaret E. Sangster
Margret Howth
Margaret Vandercook
Margaret W. Hungerford
Margret Penrose
Maria Edgeworth
Maria Thompson Daviess
Mariano Azuela
Marion Polk Angellotti
Mark Overton
Mark Twain
Mary Austin
Mary Catherine Crowley
Mary Cole
Mary Hastings Bradley
Mary Roberts Rinehart
Mary Rowlandson
M. Wollstonecraft Shelley
Maud Lindsay
Max Beerbohm
Myra Kelly
Nathaniel Hawthrone
Nicolo Machiavelli
O. F. Walton
Oscar Wilde

Owen Johnson
P.G. Wodehouse
Paul and Mabel Thorne
Paul G. Tomlinson
Paul Severing
Percy Brebner
Percy Keese Fitzhugh
Peter B. Kyne
Plato
Quincy Allen
R. Derby Holmes
R. L. Stevenson
R. S. Ball
Rabindranath Tagore
Rahul Alvares
Ralph Bonehill
Ralph Henry Barbour
Ralph Victor
Ralph Waldo Emmerson
Rene Descartes
Ray Cummings
Rex Beach
Rex E. Beach
Richard Harding Davis
Richard Jefferies
Richard Le Gallienne
Robert Barr
Robert Frost
Robert Gordon Anderson
Robert L. Drake
Robert Lansing
Robert Lynd
Robert Michael Ballantyne
Robert W. Chambers
Rosa Nouchette Carey
Rudyard Kipling
Saint Augustine
Samuel B. Allison
Samuel Hopkins Adams
Sarah Bernhardt
Sarah C. Hallowell
Selma Lagerlof
Sherwood Anderson
Sigmund Freud
Standish O'Grady
Stanley Weyman
Stella Benson
Stella M. Francis

Stephen Crane
Stewart Edward White
Stijn Streuvels
Swami Abhedananda
Swami Parmananda
T. S. Ackland
T. S. Arthur
The Princess Der Ling
Thomas A. Janvier
Thomas A Kempis
Thomas Anderton
Thomas Bailey Aldrich
Thomas Bulfinch
Thomas De Quincey
Thomas Dixon
Thomas H. Huxley
Thomas Hardy
Thomas More
Thornton W. Burgess
U. S. Grant
Upton Sinclair
Valentine Williams
Various Authors
Vaughan Kester
Victor Appleton
Victor G. Durham
Victoria Cross
Virginia Woolf
Wadsworth Camp
Walter Camp
Walter Scott
Washington Irving
Wilbur Lawton
Wilkie Collins
Willa Cather
Willard F. Baker
William Dean Howells
William le Queux
W. Makepeace Thackeray
William W. Walter
William Shakespeare
Winston Churchill
Yei Theodora Ozaki
Yogi Ramacharaka
Young E. Allison
Zane Grey